Applied Cosmobiology

A fourth revised and enlarged edition of The 90°-Dial in Practice

Reinhold Ebertin

Translated by
Heidi Langman. D.F.Astrol.S.
and
Jim ten Hove
Edited by Charles Harvey, D.F.Astrol.S.

First Printing 1972
Current Printing 2006

ISBN-10: 0-86690-086-1
ISBN-13: 978-0-86690-086-7

Cover Design: Jack Cipolla

Published by:
American Federation of Astrologers, Inc.
6535 S. Rural Road
Tempe, Arizona 85283

Printed in the United States of America

Contents

Introduction

The German edition of *The 90°-Dial in Practice* has been published several times since 1949, each time in an improved and enlarged form. I have taken this opportunity to follow the suggestion of some of my readers and have expanded the original text into a basic cosmobiology textbook under the new title of *Applied Cosmobiology*. This now covers a far wider range of material and examples than its predecessor and at the same time attempts to differentiate more clearly between traditional astrology and cosmobiology.

What then is cosmobiology? To answer this we must first of all examine the nature of astrology, for cosroobiology is undeniably rooted in genuine astrology. One of the few modern scholars to give serious attention to astrology was the late Dr. Franz Boll of Heidelberg Univ/ersity. In his view: (1)

". . . astrology, and especially Greek astrology and the closely related astrology of the Middle Ages and the Renaissance, was something different to what is commonly understood by astrology today. It was very considerably more than the mere attempt to prognosticate man's future from the 'stars'. To put it on the level with common superstition only reveals an ignorance of its essential nature and history. Astrology was a highly refined attempt at a unified world-philosophy—a philosophy of an impressive simplicity which penetrated almost every sphere of life in no less a way than for example the teaching and philosophy of Hegel. In those times to cast doubt on the fundamental truth of astrology would have been considered mistaken not only by the ignorant masses but also by the very leaders of intellectual thought themselves."

The astronomer Robert Henseling recognizes that the essential principles of astrology were based on an ancient "time conditioned" cosmobiology. He suggests (2) that ". . . the primary basis for cosmic/terrestrial relationships lies in the concept of the ecliptic and those stars in close proximity to it. This concept was based on the astro-meteorological seasons and weather lore as then understood by man in civilizations close to nature." Henseling goes on to suggest elsewhere that ". . . astro-meteorology is the earliest and most important basis for astrology. . . ." In as far as we are able to judge contemporary developments, astro-meteorology would once again seem likely to become one of the fundamentals of the new cosmobiology.

Ancient astrology was a mixture of observation, world-philosophy and religion. There is probably no religion today which does not still retain in its doctrines and rituals some part of the cosmic outlook of antiquity. However during the last two thousand years a tremendous change has taken place. Religion and science have separated, each going its own way. In the course of time astrology banished by religion and neglected by science became isolated, left to feed upon itself. The consequences of this isolation are summed up by Henseling: ". . . during the course of the centuries the originally sensible, even if to us recognizably mistaken, concept of astrology became overlaid with a dead weight of fanciful ideas and delusions. Eventually a thickly spun web of irrelevant teachings emerged, a fabric whose criss-cross intermingling threads no longer have their origins in any recognisable 'experience' but instead draw upon the desire to extend the generally accepted principle of 'As above so below' and to apply it to all and every kind of manifestation and situation. With such an objective man all too often succumbed imperceptibly to the danger of forcing the Above to accord with his picture of the Below, seeing the greater whole in every smallest detail of life and so imposing an inadequate speculation on the endless variety of man's inner and outer world and experience. . . ."

Henseling wrote this in 1941. But as early as the turn of the century a new revival of astrology was underway. Its aim was to found a new scientific astrology. However this objective could not be attained so long as the advocates of this new science were unwilling to examine and discriminate between the various component parts of this traditional mishmash of observation, philosophy and superstition.

In 1928 Dr. H.A. Strauss published the first "Jahrbuch für kosmobiologische Forschung" (3) (Cosmobiological Research Yearbook). This publication might be said to mark the establishment of the new science of cosmobiology. Like classical astrology, cosmobiology investigates relationships between the heavenly bodies and man but differs from it in its concepts and methods of investigation. Classical astrology sought through the birth horoscope to understand the individual man and his destiny in their entirety. Cosmobiology opposed this all-embracing viewpoint. Unfortunately only two issues of the "Jahrbuch für kosmobiologische Forschung" ever appeared.

In 1932 at the congress of Astrological Pioneers in Erfurt (4) I proposed that all astrological methods should be considered of equal value. Then from within this larger working context we might begin to extract those principles which appeared to be generally valid. This attempt failed. For this reason I was forced to develop a new approach myself working from both traditional and contemporary systems.

In 1938 my mother, Elsbeth Ebertin, handed over to me the annual publication "Ein Blick in die Zukunft" (A Glance into the Future), which she had founded in 1917. I transformed this into a new Cosmobiological Yearbook (5). In an article, "Kosmos-Erde-Mensch," (Universe-Earth-Man) I pointed out that the "cosmic factor" is only one of many influences which affect man. This answered many of the objections of both science and religion. For it was made absolutely clear that there was no question of the "star" having an imperative influence or of imposing an unalterable and predictable fate.

In the course of time the following factors emerged as being generally valid:

1. The zodiacal circle with its twelve signs and its division into 360° as a measuring circle.
2. The positions of the heavenly bodies in the Zodiac.
3. The angular relationships of the bodies including midpoints.
4. The rising and culminating degrees: the Ascendant and Medium Coeli.

While many followers of astrology shy away from scientific research and statistics, cosmobiology endeavours to use every type of research and methodology which can further its knowledge and help to produce more accurate results. In particular I would point to the late Prof. Tomaschek's work on earthquakes (6), and to the recent statistical work on aspects, fixed stars and galactic structures by Dr. Landscheidt (7).

The limitation in the number of interpretative factors has made it possible to develop graphs for depicting a person's overall cosmopsychological make-up, the cosmopsychogram (8), and for illustrating the transit picture for the year, evaluated as a single fluctuating curve (9). By concentrating on these factors, observation and comparisons are simplified. While in astrology the horoscope is usually considered and interpreted in isolation, it is an essential principle of cosmobiology to relate the birth picture of the individual to his general circumstances and to his environment.

No other area of science possesses cosmobiology's potential for understanding man as a whole, for comprehending his nature. And while cosmobiology uses many other sciences to check and amplify its findings, it too can be used as a most valuable tool in, for instance, psychology, psychotherapy, medicine, history, ethnology. Thus just as in antiquity there was hardly any branch of knowledge that was not nourished by astrology, so in the future cosmobiology, without becoming involved with current philosophies and ideologies, can become an invaluable aid to science.

The 90°-Dial

Each trade and profession develops suitable tools with which to ease and improve its work. The most important aid for cosmobiogical investigation is the 90°-dial. This instrument is available in three forms:

1) The universal 90°-dial. This consists of a specially designed metal drawing board base complete with a spring clamp along its upper edge. At the center of the board is a removable nut and bolt. The bolt passes through the board and through the center of the chart to be investigated. A transparent 90° calculating disc is then placed over the top of the chart and held in position with the nut. Small magnets with the birth chart factors on are used for rapid work. A transparent t-square is used with the drawing board base for work on graphic ephemeris and graphed progressions, while an adjustable t-square is used to facilitate the rapid insertion of the diagonal parallel lines used in graphing solar arc directions.

2) The standard 90°-dial. This has a stout cardboard base covered with a similar 90°chart to that on the universal dial (see Fig. 9) The calculating disc and its use on charts is identical to the universal dial.

3) The pocket 90°-dial is in the form of a soft covered wallet. On opening it one side is a small 90°-dial and on the other is a short but comprehensive booklet on its use.

These instruments are used:

1. To simplify the calculation of aspects in both the 360° and 90° circles.

2. To find mid-point configurations.

3. To determine the solar arc directions for each year of life simply by turning a second chart disc.

4. To facilitate the observation of day-to-day transits (10). (This is especially easy with the universal magnetic dial).

5. For doing synastric work for marriage partners, co-workers etc.

6. For investigating world events, current affairs etc. (11).

The following concepts are used as the basis for our work:

a) The360° zodiacal circle and its division into the 12 signs of 30° each.

b) The position of the planets. MC and Ascendant taken from the ephemeris of the relevant year and entered on the 360° chart.

c) The 90° circle used with the calculating disc to facilitate calculations.

d) The aspects of the individual factors, i.e., the angular relationships of the factors with each other as showing their mutual interaction.

In the past emphasis has tended to be placed on the following aspects:

Conjunction 0° elongation, symbol: ☌
Opposition 180° elongation, symbol: ☍
Square 90° elongation, symbol: □
Trine 120° elongation, symbol: △
Sextile 60° elongation, symbol: ⚹

At the same time there has been a tendency to play down the aspects of:

Sesquiquadrate 135° elongation, symbol: ⚼
Semi-square 45° elongation, symbol: ∠

However, experience supported by statistical evidence shows that the 45° and 135° aspects are in fact of great importance. Their neglect probably occurred because of the relative difficulty in seeing these aspects in a normal chart. Using the 90°-dial these aspects can be recognized immediately. If the arrow of the calculating disc is placed on a factor the 45° and 135° angle points are found situated on exactly the opposite side of the disc.

Over the years I have come to the conclusion that all angles divisible by 45° can be considered of virtually equal value. In the very large number of examples analyzed in our journals I have always found angles of 45° to be highly important even when only aspecting a mid-point. I would recommend that to begin with users of the 90°-dial should concentrate on those angles which are readily recognisable with the instrument: the conjunction, semi-square, square, sesquiquadrate and opposition. Later when the dial has been mastered other angular contacts can be examined.

Although in the past great significance has always been attributed to the sextile and trine I cannot reconcile this with my own experience. As I have said elsewhere on many occasions my repeated experience has been that sextiles and trines seem to relate to more passive conditions whilst those angles divisible by 45° appear to point to the actual manifestation of events.

e) The mid-point configurations. These can only be recognized easily with the use of the calculating disc on the 90° circle.

Mid-points are different from other aspects in that there have to be at least three factors involved, one of which has to be at the center of the other two. In the illustration, M represents the center of the circle and points a, b, c the positions of the planets. On the circle b is in the center of a and c and therefore the angles a-M-b and b-M-c are equal.

It will be seen that if we add the longitudes of a and c and then halve this sum that we will get the position of b. This is why mid-points are also known as half-sums since (a + c) : 2 = b.

From this we can see that direct mid-points can be fairly easily recognized if the planets involved are not too far from one another. However the recognition of the indirect mid-points is much more difficult. With these the central factor may be absent. Its place is then taken by an angular relationship to another planet. In other words a planet may be square, semi-square or sesquiquadrate to the actual mid-point. The 90°-dial is of course absolutely essential for, seeing these relationships. After even a short study the reader will see the great value of both direct and indirect midpoints, as he looks up their meanings in *The Combination of Stellar Influences* (CSI (12).

Terminology

In traditional astrology the term planets is used loosely to include the Sun and the Moon. This is of course not strictly correct and so we therefore usually use the term stellar bodies or just bodies. If we want to include the Medium Coeli, Ascendant and the Moon's Node we will then use the term factors.

The Evolution of the 90°-Dial

In the course of time a fundamental change has taken place in the presentation of the birth chart, horoscope or cosmogram.

A square horoscope has been handed down to us from the Middle Ages. An example of this is Fig. 1, the chart of Wallenstein as calculated by Kepler. At this time the main basis for interpretation was the division of the horoscope into the twelve mundane houses. Each house corresponded to a certain sphere of human activity. Here the parental home is represented by the fourth; wealth, fifth; illness, sixth; marriage, seventh; and so on. In this maze of triangles the mutual relationship of all the factors can only be seen with the greatest difficulty.

Fig. 2 shows a form of chart presentation in which the mundane circle, not the zodiac, is divided into twelve houses as a basis for interpretation. The cusps are marked with the positions they occupy on the ecliptic and it will be quickly seen that these houses are of unequal size. Presented in this way it is still far from easy to recognize the angular relationships between the various factors. Surprisingly this method of chart presentation was still in use in Germany as late as 1930. Its use persists to this day abroad, especially in the U.S.A.

The difficulties that arise when using this type of map are especially noticeable when calculating directions and transits, where specific distances have to be determined. For such work only the sign and degree division of the zodiacal circle are a useful basis for work. When in 1928 I began the regular publication of a journal, known today as *Kosmobiologie* (13), I used the zodiacal circle di-

Fig. 1 The horoscope of Wallenstein calculated by Johannes Kepler shows the square representation. The main point was to grasp the positions of the planets within the twelve houses.

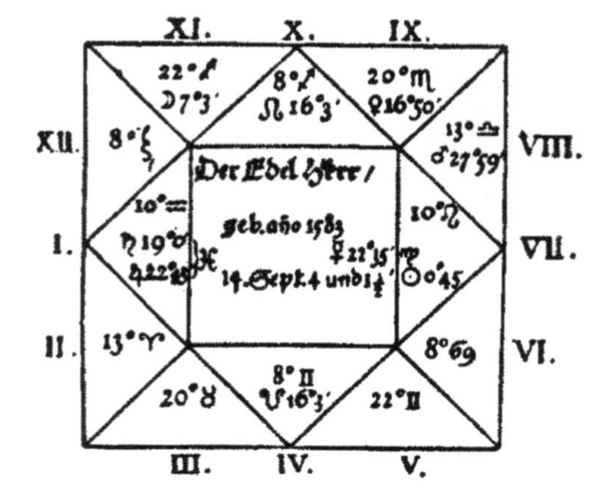

Fig. 2 The horoscope of Rudolf Steiner, according to Libra's *Astrologie, ihre Technik und Ethik*, Ammersfoort/Holland, 1915. A circular presentation is preferred, but the houses form the foundation. The cusps are entered on the outside. According to the drawing, the houses appear equal in size, but are in fact not so. The first house has 30°, the second 34°, the third 36°, etc. Here, a lot of practice is needed to work out transits or directions.

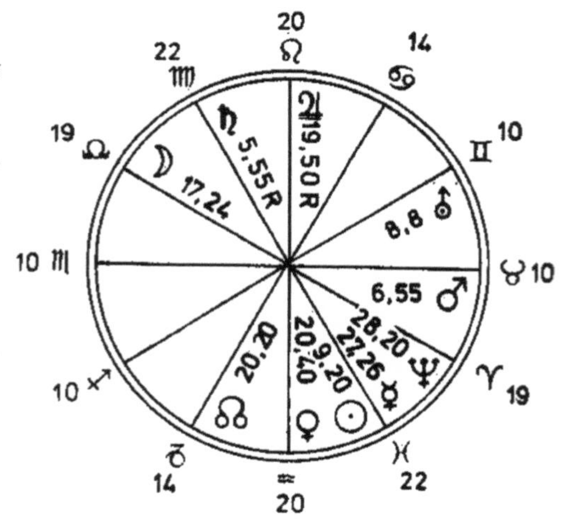

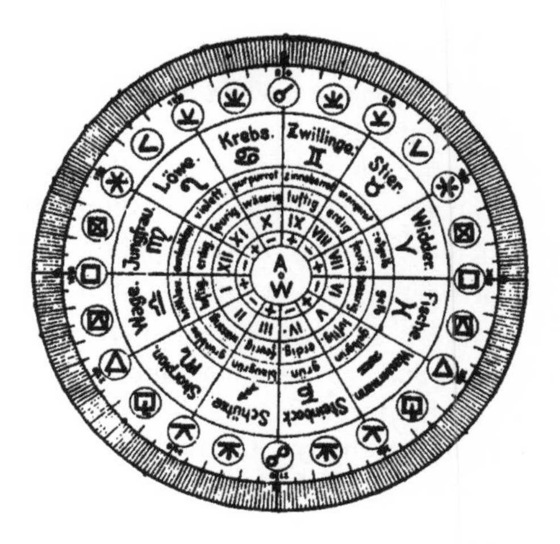

Fig. 3 Witte-Degree-Disc, reduced. The original is 15cm in diameter.

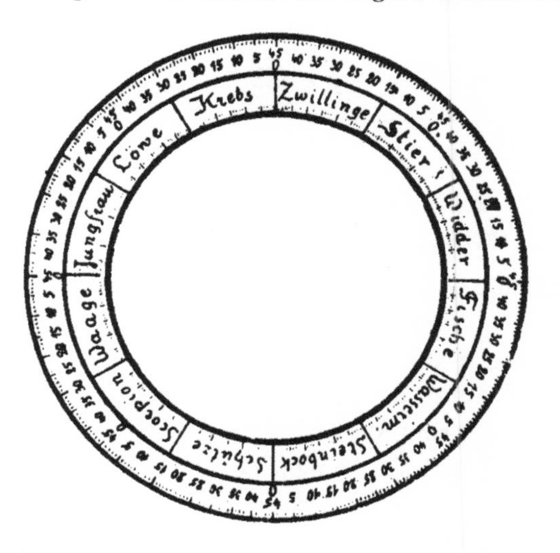

Fig. 4 Calculating Table for the 45°-system. Table for calculating positions in the 45°-system. For this purpose one has to look for the position of the planet in the zodiac and will find the number for the 45°-dial at the outer circle. Examples: A planet in 5°Aries in the zodiac means 5° on the 45°-dial. 10° Taurus means 40°. 7° Gemini means 22°. 13°34' Sagittarius means 20°34' on the dial.

vided into degrees for all work from the outset.

It was a revolutionary act when Alfred Witte (14) discarded the zodiac altogether and used instead the degree disc shown in Fig, 3. He placed this disc on a sheet of paper, drew a circle around it, marked 0° Cancer as zero and then entered the various factors round the outside. This disc, fastened in the center with a drawing pin, was used to calculate the angular distances and mid-points.

However this type of work had two drawbacks. Once one moved or turned the disc the connection with the zodiac was completely lost. Furthermore the degree markings were so close together that it was extremely difficult to place the disc accurately. If the center moved only slightly a discrepancy of several degrees resulted at the circumference.

Alfred Witte placed the main emphasis on those angles which result from a progressive division of the circle by two:

360° : 2 = 180° = opposition
180° : 2 = 90° = square
90° : 2 = 45° = semi-square

This gave him the idea of constructing a 90° disc which would cover all these angular relationships.

Since the sign Aries is in opposition to the sign Libra and both these are square to Cancer and Capricorn, all these signs are placed on top of one another in the first 30° of the 90°-circle. Repeating this idea, Taurus, Leo, Scorpio and Aquarius are placed together in the next 30°, from 30° to 60°, and the signs Gemini, Virgo, Sagittarius, Pisces follow from 60° to 90°. Witte also invented a 45°-circle, for which he divided the circle into eight sectors, the positions being distributed on the 45°-circle on a similar basis to that used for the 90°-circle. Fig. 4 is the table which I designed at that time for calculating positions in the 45°-system. Figs. 5 and 6 show Goethe's birth chart according to the 360° and 45° systems. These illustrations are intended for general orientation only, for in practice the 45°-circle has not proved very satisfactory. It so readily

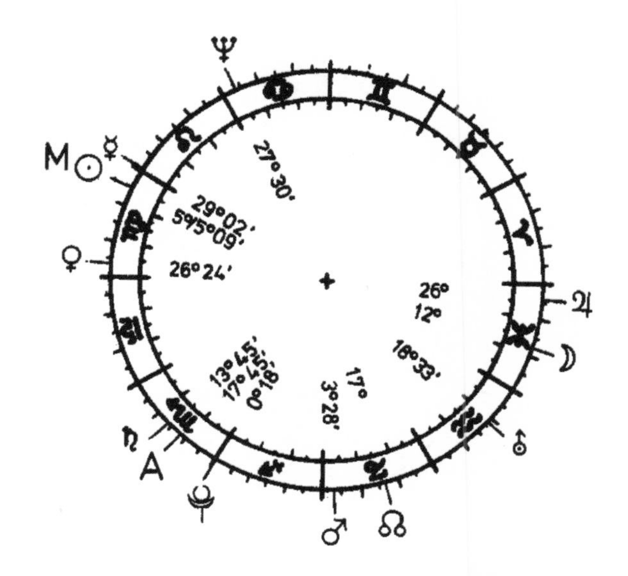

Fig. 5 Goethe's birth chart according to the 360° system.

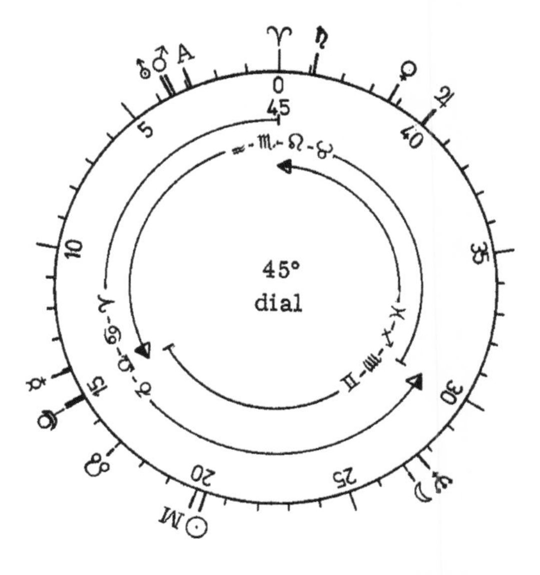

Fig. 6 Goethe's birth chart according to the 45° system.

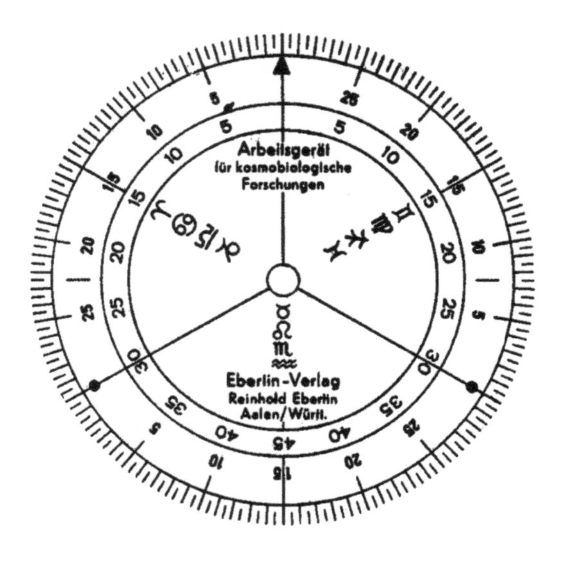

Fig. 7 Disc of the 90°-dial.

leads to involvement with angles of 22.5° and these have not been confirmed in the same way as other aspects. Apart from this the transfer of individual positions from 360° to 90° is considerably simpler so that fewer mistakes are likely to creep in. However the 45°-system has proved most useful for the construction of graphic ephemerides (15). These valuable additions to the 90°-dial will be discussed later.

To begin with work with the 90°-dial will be unfamiliar. The accompanying conversion table for every 5° will be of help. An expanded version giving conversions for every degree into both 90° and 45°-circles is given at the back of the book. To convert a position enter the table at the appropriate zodiacal longitude and trace across to the end column where the equivalent value will be found, e.g., a planet in 10° Leo is found to have a value of 40° in the right hand column and must therefore be entered at 40° on the 90°-circle. A planet in 25° Pisces will be entered at 85° and so on.

If we now compare the degree markings in Figs. 3 and 7 the superior clarity and accuracy of the 90°-system for calculations can be plainly seen.

Conversion Table

00 Aries	00 Cancer	00 Libra	00 Capricorn	= 00
05	05	05	05	= 05
10	10	10	10	= 10
15	15	15	15	= 15
20	20	20	20	= 20
25	25	25	25	= 25
00 Taurus	00 Leo	00 Scorpio	00 Aquarius	= 30
05	05	05	05	= 35
10	10	10	10	= 40
15	15	15	15	= 45
20	20	20	20	= 50
25	25	25	25	= 55
00 Gemini	00 Virgo	00 Sagittarius	00 Pisces	= 60
05	05	05	05	= 65
10	10	10	10	= 70
15	15	15	15	= 75
20	20	20	20	= 80
25	25	25	25	= 85
30	30	30	30	= 90

On the calculating dial shown in Fig. 7 there are two distinct scales. The outer scale is marked off in three consecutive runs of 30° each corresponding to the cardinal, fixed and mutable signs as marked. The inner scale is marked from 0°- 45° in both directions from the indicator arrow. It is this second scale which is used for noting factors that are equidistant from any point. This essential second scale is the only one marked on the calculating disc of the full-size 90°-dial, which however also has lines marked for noting the aspects in the 360°-circle. See lower half of Fig, 28. The smaller pocket version of the dial retains both.

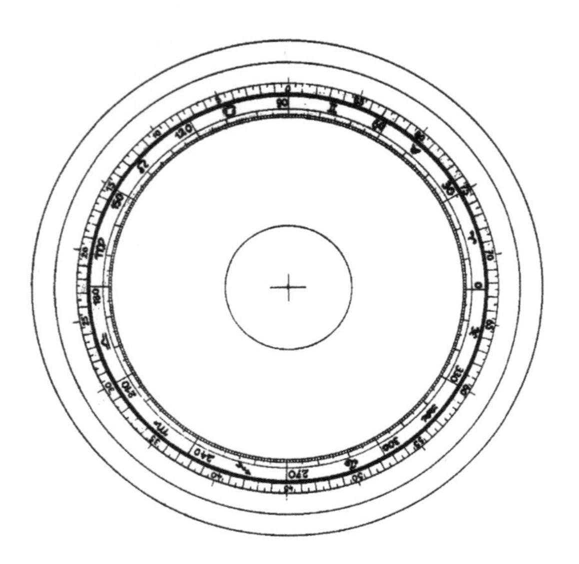

Fig. 8 Reduced K2 chart from called K1

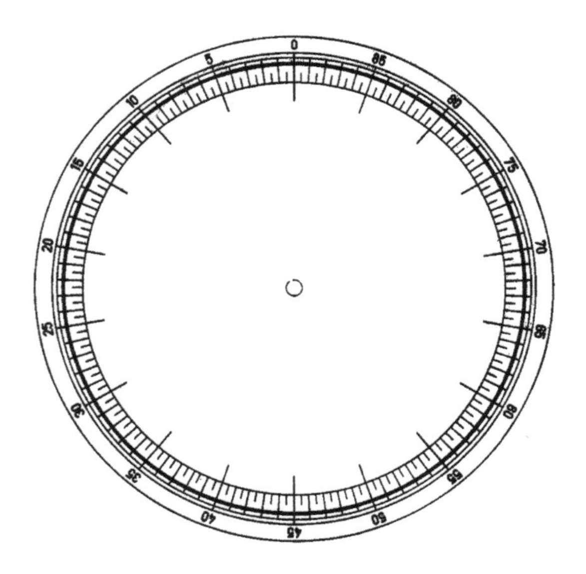

Fig. 9 90°-Dial for Cosmobiological Research

The Chart Form

The writer designed the K2 chart form especially for use with the 90°-dial. The K is from the German word Kombination as the chart form combines both the 360° and the 90°-circles. The 360°-circle is divided into the twelve signs and differs from other chart forms only in so far as that all additional markings have been left off. At one time the more important fixed stars were marked. These are now omitted because of their large numbers and the fact that some stars are so far from the ecliptic that they cannot in fact form conjunctions with any of the planets. Sun or Moon. More details on this matter can be found in *Fixed Stars* by Ebertin & Hoffmann (16).

Fig. 8 shows the smaller K1 chart form. We have kept all the example charts to this same size throughout. In this way the reader can, by cutting out the example disc. Fig. 7, and stiffening it with card, follow the examples through with the explanations and commentary given.

Fig. 10 is the birth chart of Goethe. This has been chosen as an example because the life and work of this great German poet are probably familiar to most people.

An unfamiliar requirement of this new approach is that the zodiacal circle is always placed in the same position with 0°Cancer at the top. Everything has to be entered so that it is readable from one viewpoint. We must therefore forego the usual habit of always placing the Ascendant to the left and the MC at the top. Though this will at first seem very strange, this method gives us the big advantage that individual cosmograms can be easily compared and the transiting planets entered in the same place. This loss of the mundane houses will be found to be outweighed by many advantages, which can only be appreciated by regular work with the 90°-dial.

When entering the symbols in the 360° circle the K2 chart remains upright. It should not be rotated. The symbols should be entered in such a way that they can be read easily when the chart is in its normal upright position. When the symbols have been entered the degree positions can be written in. These should read to or from the center of the circle as shown in the example charts. Here if is unavoidable to rotate the chart slightly but the positions of the individual factors should be made readable without having to turn the chart.

When completing the 90°-circle it is as well to start by first marking in the positions of all the factors with a dash. Then if there should happen to be amassing of factors at anyone point the symbols can be entered clearly. All the symbols should be written facing into the centre of the circle so that when the dial has to be turned in the course of work the symbols on the outer 90° circle always remain in an upright position. The importance of always entering all symbols clearly and precisely, exactly on the right degree cannot be overemphasized. By being absolutely accurate the work of calculating the aspects and mid-points is made considerably easier. Some have found it easier to mark the positions of the planets in the 90°-circle with a line and then set the symbol next it. This is not recommended. In the cases of Mercury, Venus, Jupiter, Saturn, Neptune and Pluto it is best to use the upright which forms part of the symbols as a marker. For this reason the Pluto symbol with the central leg is used. In the cases of Sun, Moon, Mars, Uranus, Moon's Node, Asc and MC it is advisable to write the symbol over a short marker line. If the positions are entered in this way it is possible to obtain an accuracy of 10/4 in calculations.

Some readers will no doubt consider this detailed introduction pedantic. In reality this is not so. When working with the 90°-dial it is first and foremost the eye that is used. Mutual relationships have to be recognized visually before one begins their calculation. Anyone who follows this system will in a short while be able to recognize the essential points of a cosmogram and be able to make an immediate diagnosis. Such rapid assessment has not been possible previously with other methods in this field.

When transferring the positions from the 360°-circle to the 90°-circle it is easiest to start with the signs Aries, Cancer, Libra, Capricorn. Any factors in these signs are entered in the first 30°-sector, top left. Therefore in our example of Goethe, Fig. 10, Mars in 3°28' Capricorn will be marked at the top left at 3°28'. Next the Moon's Node at 17° Capricorn will be entered in 17° of the same sector, then Neptune at 27°30' Cancer is placed at 27°30'.

Next we look for any factors in Taurus, Leo, Scorpio, Aquarius. These will have to be entered in the lower sector between 30° and 60°. Saturn is in 13°45' Scorpio corresponding to 43°45', while Asc in 17°45' Scorpio is in almost identical position with Uranus in 18°33' Aquarius corresponding to 47°45' and 48°33' respectively. Mercury in 29° Leo will be placed in 59°.

Finally the factors in Gemini, Virgo, Sagittarius and Pisces are dealt with. Pluto in 0° Sagittarius is placed at 60°. The Sun and MC both at about 5° Virgo are entered at 65°, the Moon in 12° Pisces goes to 72°, Jupiter in 26° Pisces and Venus in 25°24' Virgo are entered at 86° and 86°24',

(The chart could of course be converted equally well by taking each quadrant in turn. Starting with Aries any factors therein would be entered in the 0°-30° sector. Next any factors in Taurus would be put in the 30°-60° sector. Then the positions in Gemini would be dealt with. Continuing in this way in the next quadrant Cancer position = 0°-30°, Leo = 30°-60° and Virgo = 60°-90° and so on through the third and fourth quadrants. The result is the same either way.)

If we now study Fig. 10 as a whole and compare the two circles,

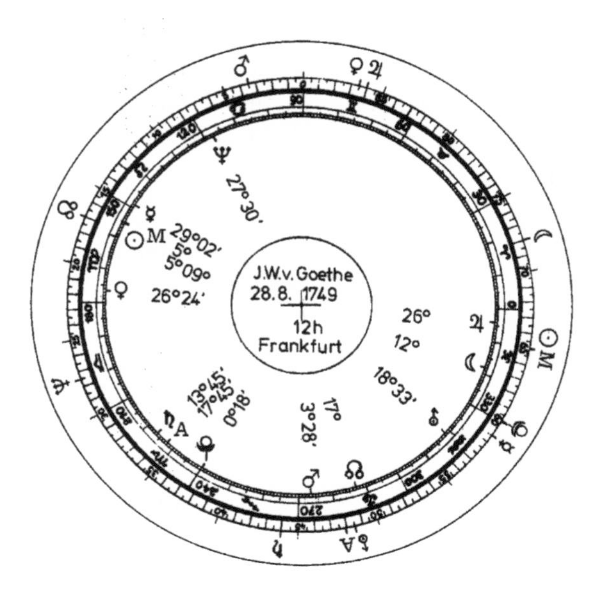

Fig. 10 Goethe's birth chart; 360°-circle inside; 90°-circle outside

it will be seen that at no point do these two circles coincide. Each circle must always be used quite separately. At times several factors may seem to be at the same point in both Circles. For example we have Jupiter in 20° Pisces and the Sun in 65° on the 90°-circle. These two however must not be compared. The 90°-circle is our calculating circle, an aid for the analysis of the 360° inner circle. We must always remember that these two circles do not have any points of contact and must be treated quite independently of each other.

In the 90°-circle we see clusters of factors. These are in mutual angular relationship. For example in the 90°-circle Venus and Jupiter are seen to be close together. In the 360°-circle they are in opposition. Mercury and Pluto are conjoined in the 90°-circle but 90° apart in the 360°-circle. In the 90°-circle Uranus and the Ascendant arc both in about 48° with Mars exactly opposite them. In the 360o-circle Uranus is square to the Ascendant with Mars

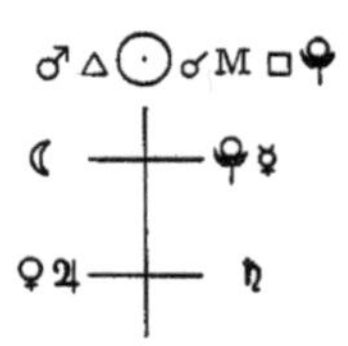

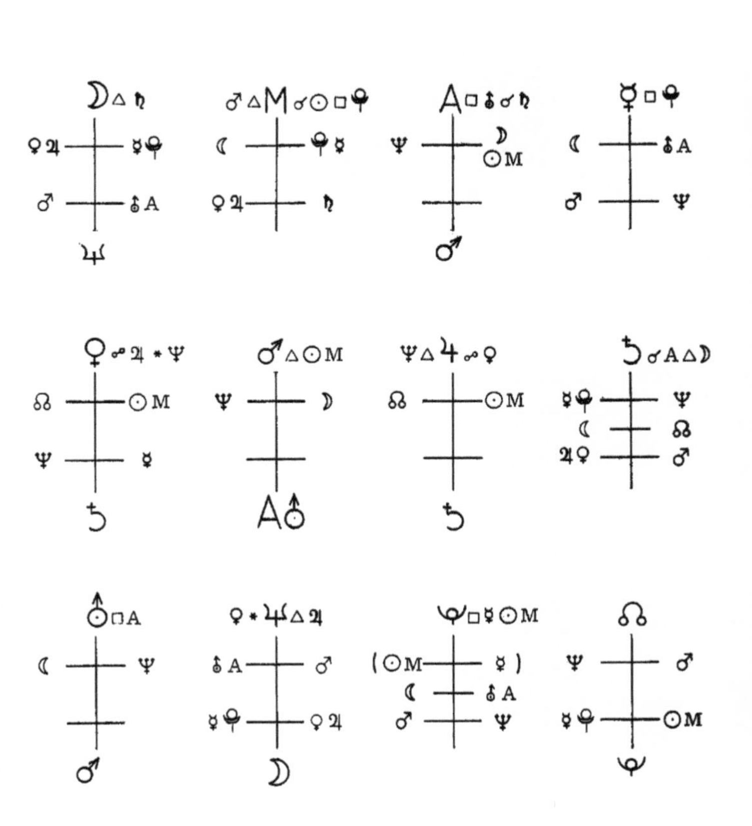

Fig. 11

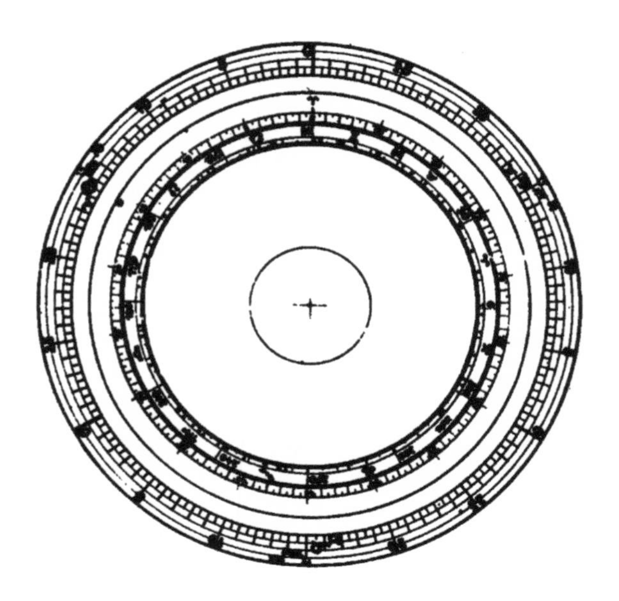

Fig. 12 The old cork dial in reduced size

semi-square to both. Already then we find here an angular relationship which would not he easily recognisable without the dial.

One might wonder if it would not be better to mark the factors in the 90°-circle with their sign positions. This was in fact done with an earlier version of the dial shown in Fig.12. The chart was glued to a cork disc. The dial consisted of four rings, each ring corresponding to one sign. Using this it was possible to enter the positions of the factors In the appropriate sign in the 90°-circle.

This method did not in fact prove very satisfactory but it may be found of great help when first using the dial.

Interpreting the Birth Chart

To prepare the chart for analysis on the dial it must first be cut out from the form along the second outside circle. Then placing the transparent disc exactly over the top of the chart ensure that all the degree markings on the disc are in exactly identical positions with those on the chart, and that the arrow indicator of the disc points to 0° Cancer. Now using the dial as a punch press the bolt from underneath, up through the hole in the dial and through the chart. If the hole is not absolutely central the first time the paper will tear a little. In this event, after ensuring that the cut out form is now exactly central, linen stiffening rings can be stuck on either side of the form to reinforce it.

The chart is now ready for analysis. But before we begin I wish to make it clear once again that these birth patterns are only as it were the cosmic impress.

The cosmic factor is only one of many which help to shape the nature and fate of man. Heredity, environment, the parental home, the contemporary economic conditions and in particular one's own will, all play a part in molding the course our life will take.

The character delineation based on cosmic principles is primarily derived from the configurations within the zodiacal circle. The dial is only used to enable us to recognize these details more quickly and easily. The cosmic factors correlate primarily with the human psyche. The basis of all these interpretations is therefore cosmo-psychology. The two main works of reference used are: *Kosmo-psychologie* (17) and *The Combination of Stellar Influences* (abbreviated CSI).

This book does not use any system of house division for interpretation or forecasting. While the disagreement over house division would seem to be settled now that Dr. Theodor Landscheidt (18) has shown that statistically only Dr. Koch's system shows significant reactions for individual house cusps, this does not mean that the traditional meaning of the houses has been proved. What we do know is that the traditional interpretations such as "Saturn in the second means a life of poverty," "Jupiter in the eighth indicates a large inheritance," or "Neptune in the seventh brings an unhappy marriage" just do not hold good.

By using such methods of interpretation we are not only likely to draw wrong conclusions but more important we are likely to impose an unnecessary burden on the person for whom these things have been foretold creating anxiety and neurosis. But this aside one can demonstrate that in countless examples this method of interpretation just is not confirmed by the facts. The need to adhere to those principles which rest on a solid foundation of fact cannot be stressed too often.

Nearly fifty years experience has led me to the principle that: Only those factors are useful which have proved themselves in prognosis.

By this I am not denying the value of studying past events and happenings. One can learn much from such work. But experience gained in this way will need to be demonstrated again and again before it can be considered valid. One must repeatedly try making forecasts. Even if one is proved wrong it is still a most useful exercise. And if a prognosis is correct then one should investigate the relationship between it and the incorrect forecast. To publish only confirmative examples is highly unsatisfactory.

The individual points in a birth chart are:

M = MC = The Medium Coeli and its opposite the Imum Coeli

A = AS = The Ascendant and its opposite the descendant.

These are known as the individual points because they move

about one degree in four minutes. With the aid of the dial these points can be rectified and the' precise time of birth confirmed. In the past the Ascendant was usually considered to be the most important individual factor. Now more and more the even greater importance of the MC, is becoming evident. The Ascendant is dependent upon the MC. We first calculate the MC and then extract the Ascendant from a set of tables.

The ascending degree is the degree of the ecliptic rising on the eastern horizon at the time of birth, the apparent meeting point of ecliptic and horizon. We live and move on the horizontal plane and in a way the individual's Ascendant can be seen as the point of contact with other people and the mutual relationship between the individual and his environment. For the environment helps to shape the individual and the individual leaves his mark upon his surroundings. However it would seem mistaken to identify character with the Ascendant. The Ascendant seems to correlate much more with Jung's use of the term "persona" in its sense of a mask in which a person appears and through which a person plays a part in the world.

The MC on the other hand seems to relate to the actual inner life, to my own ego, including my inner ambitions and will to make my own decisions. It is the ego that feels a sense of independent being when related to other human beings. This strong sense of ego-consciousness seems to have only really developed in man in the last 500 years, and is interestingly paralleled in painting by the development of the three dimensional viewpoint and the art of perspective. During this recent period man has had to learn more and more to experience himself as an independent being apart from the tribe and the community. (See Gebser*'s Ursprung und Gegenwart* (19)). This development helps to explain why in ancient times the Ascendant was considered more important than the Medium Coeli. This apparent digression into psychology at this point is deliberate. To study cosmobiology without psychology is impossible. It is hoped that these ideas will stimulate readers to study psychology further.

The ability to read a cosmogram is absolutely essential for everyone who uses the 90°-dial. However the novelty of the method presented here does need thorough explanation.

In Goethe's birth chart Sun and MC are in conjunction; that is, the Sun is culminating. Goethe said he was born in Frankfurt as the clock was showing correct local time; we will investigate later whether this moment in time does in fact coincide with the awakening of life. It is said that the infant Goethe was apparently dead when born. But the mid-wife had made a mistake and, so the story goes, on discovering her error the house resounded to the cry "He's alive!" It is possible the birth did take place on the stroke of noon, but the first cry, the moment of incarnation, was a little later.

Before examining all the complex combinations of factors it is advisable to first study the cosmic condition of the individual factors. By the cosmic condition of a factor we mean its position in the zodiac and its many relationships to other factors. The following scheme is suggested:

A. Zodiacal position: ☉ in ♍
B. Aspect relationships: ☉ ☌ MC
C. Mid-points: ☉ = ♀/♄ = ♃/♄

The aspects do not of course have to be exact to the degree. A certain deviation or orb is allowed.. In the book *Die kosmischen Grundlagen unseres Lebens* we adopted the following orbs:

Personal points: (Sun, Moon, MC, AS) = 5°
Fast moving planets: (Mercury, Venus, Mars) = 4°
Slow moving planets: (Jupiter. Saturn, Uranus, Neptune, Pluto) and the Moon's Node = 3°

The orbs of traditional astrology where orbs of up to 15° are sometimes allowed does not seem acceptable to us. Our approach is that personal, individual points deserve a larger orb, the slow moving or heavy planets a small orb since their positions are much the same for very many people, while the faster moving planets should be placed somewhere between the two as they do have a certain personal value.

Accordingly the Sun conjunct MC is considered as exact, the Sun square Pluto just makes it with a 5° orb, and the Sun trine Mars in within 2°.

Next the dial is used to calculate the mid-points. The arrow of the transparent disc is set to the point under investigation on the 90° circle, in this instance the Sun. The scale on the disc running in both directions makes it easy to read the distances on either side of the Sun. An orb of only one and a half degrees is allowed for mid-points. Examining the Sun axis we find that on one side the distance to the Moon is about 7°, while on the other Pluto is 5° away and Mercury 6°. At the same time we see that Venus and Jupiter are 22° to one side and Saturn 23° the other. We therefore have the following mid-point picture for the Sun: Sun = Moon/Mercury = Moon/Pluto = Venus/Saturn = Jupiter/Saturn.

When writing mid-points it is best to write the faster moving planet first. Thus above we have Moon/Mercury, Venus/Saturn etc. because this is the order that is used *in The Combination of Stellar Influences* (CSI), and this will make looking up the combinations that much simpler. An exception to this order is that the Sun, as a primary factor, is placed before the Moon. The personal points MC and AS are placed at the end.

The angular relationships of the mid-points can be checked on the 360°circle by placing the arrow of the disc on the factor under investigation and using the 45°, 90° and 135° aspect lines marked on the center of the disc (see Fig. 28). Placing the arrow of the disc on the Sun it is hard to see that the Sun, Mercury and Moon are in mutual relationship. But if we now look at the lines marking the square aspects and treat these as center points or axes we will See that the Moon and Mercury are the same distance either side. So to be precise we should write: Sun square Moon/Mercury.

In the case of Sun = Moon/Pluto the relationship is even more difficult to see. Keeping the arrow on the Sun it can be seen that the sesquiquadrate marking is in the center of Moon/Pluto. Once again to be precise we should write: Sun sesquiquadrate Moon/Pluto.

Some time ago in my suggestions for an International Nomenclature (20) I proposed that we use the appropriate number of degrees for indicating aspects by simply connecting the factors to the number with a hyphen.

For Sun sesquiquadrate Moon/Pluto one would write: Sun-135-Moon/Pluto. Sun semi-square Venus/Saturn would be written: Sun-45-Venus /Saturn. Sun sesquiquadrate Jupiter/Saturn would be written as Sun-135-Jupiter/Saturn.

One should differentiate between direct mid-points, where a factor is at half the distance between two others as for instance Mars = Uranus/AS, and indirect mid-points where a factor forms an aspect to the mid-point of two other factors as for example Sun = 45-Venus/Saturn.

When first using the 90°circle it is as well to check all results obtained on the inner 360°circle.

All the angles divisible by 45° are easily recognizable on the 90° circle but difficulties may arise when calculating sextiles (60°) and trines (120°). For these aspects instead of the arrow the 30°marks on the calculating disc are placed on the factor to be examined. For example in Goethe's chart if one places the right hand 30° marking of the disc on Venus and Jupiter it will be seen that the arrow will indicate those points which form an angle with it divisible by 30°. In the example the arrow points to Neptune. If we examine the inner 360°circle we see that Neptune is 120° from Jupiter and 60° from Venus.

Placing the left-hand 30° mark of the disc on Venus and Jupiter the arrow falls on Mercury. Here we find Mercury-60-Venus and Mercury-150-Jupiter. The question now arises as to which of these aspects we include in our analysis? My own experience has been that the angles divisible by 45° give the best results. In general I have managed with only these angles. And I would recommend that to begin with the student confines himself to, these angles and only later adds the other aspects. Otherwise there is a danger of becoming confused by the profusion of other aspects and arriving at the wrong conclusions. It should be kept in mind that progress has mainly been made in cosmobiology by reducing the number of factors. This of course does not exclude other factors from diagnosis and prognosis so long as their effects and actions are convincingly demonstrated, as in the case of the recent work of Dr. Landscheidt and Professor Tomaschek (21).

The next thing we need to know is whether there are any other mid-point contacts or whether we have perhaps allowed too large an orb for those we have. It is essential to be precise with these calculations. As a practical aid the little "Astro-Addiator" machine is recommended (22), as it both saves time and excludes a possible source of error.

Let us choose as an example the direct mid-point Mercury Venus/ Neptune. Anyone finding difficulty in calculating the planets positions in zodiacal longitude from 0°Aries is referred to the Table of Equivalents for 360°, 90° and 4 5° Calculating Systems at the end of the illustrations section of this book.

From this we find:

Venus	= 26°24' Virgo	= 176°24'
Neptune	= 27°30' Cancer	= 117°30'
Venus + Neptune		= 293°54'
Venus/Neptune		= 146°57'
Venus/Neptune = 26°57' Leo		

This is written as:

Mercury = Venus/Neptune
29°02' Leo = 26°57' Leo

As a help in these conversions the distances from 0°Aries are given for the beginning of each sign on our chart forms. Thus if as here the sign position of a mid-point at 146°57' is required take the next lowest position marked = 120° = 0° Leo and subtract this to get the position. Here we have 146°57 - 120° = 26°57' Leo.

The difference is more than 2° and we will therefore have to decide whether or not to include this mid-point. This will be decided later when we are interpreting the planetary aspects.

The calculation of the indirect mid-points is very similar. Calculating Sun = Moon/Mercury we have the following:

Moon	= 12°00' Pisces	= 342°00'
Mercury	= 29°02' Leo	= 149°02'
Moon + Mercury		= 491°02'
Moon/Mercury		= 245°31'
Moon/Mercury = 5°31' Sagittarius		

The Sun in 5°09 Virgo is therefore square Moon/Mercury.

Next let us calculate the position of Sun at the mid-point of Venus/Saturn:

Saturn	= 13°45' Scorpio	= 223°45'
Venus	= 26°24' Virgo	= 176°24'
Venus + Saturn		= 400°09'
Venus/Saturn		= 200°04'
Venus/Saturn = 20°04' Libra		

Thus the Venus/Saturn, mid-point is semi-square the Sun.

It is also possible to calculate the mid-points directly in terms of the 90°circle. The preceding example could then read:

Venus	= 26°24' Virgo	= 86°24'
Saturn	= 13°45' Scorpio	= 43°45'
Venus + Saturn		= 130°09'
Venus/Saturn		= 65° 04'

We should note here that there are of course always two mid-points exactly opposite each other. If we draw the diameter from 65° of the 90°circle it will cut the opposite side of the circle at 20°, corresponding to the result of 20° Libra which we obtained above.

In order to get a general picture of a cosmogram the cosmic condition of all the factors; is first computed with the help of the dial. Even better is to draw up the structural elements of the chart as shown in Fig. 11. With a little practice this overall picture can be set up in about 5 minutes. For convenience and clarity it is best to use the KS 2 chart form for this.

This specially designed chart form is large enough for entering on the structural elements and then adding in the appropriate notes from CSI alongside (preferably typed). By using these a convenient resume of facts can be made that will always be useful either for a short analysis or for a quick assessment of the basic factors when studying transits and directions.

If you are not certain whether to a allow a particular midpoint, the arrow of the dial may be moved up to 1½° to either side, but you should not allow larger orbs than this. Orbs of 3° are too large. But let us not quarrel over such rules! It is far better to experiment for yourself. Preferably not with your own chart! We tend to be prejudiced about our own charts! Nevertheless you will not always agree with the writer's viewpoint for there must always be points on which there can be a difference of opinion. Here in the structural elements of Goethe's chart, Fig.11, under Pluto. (Sun, MC/Mercury) has been put in brackets. This is because a larger orb than usual has been allowed. Interpreting these particular points one has to admit that they do correlate in the main with Goethe's nature. Thus there are borderline cases.

Once the technical analysis of the chart has been completed the work of interpretation proper can begin. Those who are just beginning the study of birth charts will have to copy the meanings of the individual combinations from CSI.

(In recent editions of CSI each statement in the book has been numbered. It would therefore suffice if the appropriate CSI number were noted next to each combination. However if the reader were to look up all the numbered paragraphs first he could easily lose sight of the general picture and so for this reason shortened versions of each combination have been given here.)

Sun = MC: individuality, objective in life individual advancement, individual relationships.

Sun = Moon/Mercury: biological thinking, good intellectual powers, realistic thinking.

MC = Moon/Mercury: independent thinking, search for soul contacts, forming one's own judgement.

Sun = Moon/Pluto: a sensitive nature, excitability.

MC = Moon/Pluto: very tense emotional life, one-sidedness, the inclination to act alone, not in accord with other people.

Sun = Venus/Saturn: dissatisfaction, inhibitions in sex (love) expression, unhealthy expression of the sex-urge, weak procreative powers.

MC = Venus/Saturn: inhibitions in sex (love) expression, dissatisfaction, irritability, jealousy, reserve, seeking solitude.

Sun = Jupiter/Saturn: inconstancy, moodiness (through illness, e.g., disturbance of the liver's function).

MC = Jupiter/Saturn: desire for solitude, inhibitions, love of loneliness and seclusion, the philosopher.

Sun trine Mars: energy, determination, perseverance, ambition, diligence, a desire to lead and for power, obstinacy, stubbornness, restlessness.

MC trine Mars: ego-conscious action, decisive, consciousness of one's aims and objectives in life, independence, prudence, rashness, impulsiveness.

Sun square Pluto: striving for power by means of physical and mental energy, consciousness of aim or objectives in life, creative powers, appreciation of innovations, talent for leadership, overestimation of self, arrogance.

MC square Pluto: shaping of individuality, desire to become important. the unfoldment of strength, power to succeed, organization. prudence, vision, authority, foolhardiness, licentiousness.

Such notes will inevitably contain contradictions. These should always be included as so often these contradictions will in fact be found to be present. On the other hand interpretations of a similar meaning will often recur, indicating those tendencies which are of greater importance. In CSI I point out that the interpretations given are only suggested points for consideration and that these should not be expected in any way to correlate word for word with the actual circumstances. CSI should not be treated as a book of rules but rather as a guide to Interpretation. It is always pleasing when one obtains results that are according to the book, but this cannot always be expected to be the case. CSI has often been dubbed a lazy-bones which it is not intended to be. Yet it is desirable to have certain fundamental guidelines for reference and comparison.

If we now sum up the main points derived from the positions of the Sun and MC in Goethe's chart we might say:

Here we have a man whose individuality distinguishes him from the general run. A man who through his intellectual ability will arrive at independent judgement and opinions, who will distinguish himself through his readiness for action, determination, energy, resolution and his consciousness of his objectives in life. A nature that has vision and prudence, organizing ability, and who ego-consciously goes his own way, who achieves influence and importance and authority on account of his qualities of leadership. At times he will retire seeking solitude, showing himself to be sensitive and dissatisfied, he is subject to psychic tension which others may term moodiness and inconstancy. At times he can be arrogant and licentious.

If we now also consider Goethe's home background, how he grew up, his childhood associates, his educational opportunities, and how much he was generally helped in ev6ry direction, then we can understand the many characteristics that have been ascertained here from the positions of the Sun and MC in the cosmogram.

You will notice that when interpreting the aspects both the positive and negative meanings have been included. I am convinced that all combinations have both positive and negative characteristics, but blended in different proportions. One should not for example consider Sun square Saturn as wholly unfavorable. A possible tendency to rashness or premature action may be held in check by this, and rich experiences may be gained and a serious, responsible attitude to life may develop through such a position. On the other hand Jupiter-Pluto contacts which may often lead to successes can under different circumstances produce irresponsibility and rash speculation. Thus conclusions should never be drawn from one single aspect but always from a consideration of the cosmogram as a whole.

Next in importance when judging an angular relationship is the nature of the factors involved and not the type of aspect they form (23). Sextiles and trines used to be considered favorable and squares and oppositions as essentially unfavorable. However in practice it has been found that exceptional personalities only seem to develop when a chart contains fewer trines than squares and oppositions. People without these tensions appeared to be rather dull and in spite of their many trines did not achieve expected successes. It would seem that squares, oppositions and conjunctions are especially important for getting on in life and that in turn these potentialities seem to manifest themselves through similar 'tension aspects' in the directions and transits.

The Sun square Pluto in Goethe's chart confirms the aspirations for gaining a leading and privileged position. In Weimar he worked his way up to become the premier civil servant of the State, was elevated to the peerage, became a Privy Councillor, and held the chair in the Chamber. "We should not think of Goethe as a shy reserved poet uncertain of his position. He was fully conscious of his high office and could if necessary be as tough as the Duke himself." (24) Goethe's elevation to the peerage was a matter of great pride to him. "He was not in the least overawed by it. As a Frankfurt patrician's son he had always considered himself as belonging to the nobility." (25) Goethe was thus not only conscious of his important position but could at times be arrogant. But this is the negative side of his having achieved a position of power and authority.

In Goethe's cosmogram we find Venus opposition Jupiter. This definitely implies that the poet did not always behave himself correctly in matters of love. At times he could be a wastrel with very exaggerated feelings. On the other hand he had the ability to endear himself through his understanding nature. In a positive sense it is this position that depicts the artist.

However it is not possible to lay down in what proportion the positive and negative traits will be operative and it is always essential to consider the general picture of a cosmogram as well as the individual aspects. The cosmic conditions of the Sun and MC can be considered to be positive with the exception of the Venus/Saturn mid-point. But if as here we see an ambition and desire to be alone, to seek solitude and to be able to contemplate and mature, then we must also attribute a positive side to this configuration. For there are after all a great many people who learn nothing at all from life's conflicts because they do not allow themselves time to think and collect and digest their experience.

Let us now take a closer look at the Ascendant which is in conjunction with Saturn. square Uranus, semi-square Mars and in the axes of Moon/Neptune, Sun/Neptune and Neptune/MC. According to CSI these elements may be interpreted as follows:

Saturn conjunct AS: feelings of inhibition, frustration

Uranus square AS: quick response to the influences of the environment. An unstable, quickly responding and original personality, a love of change, inventive ability, connections with technology. An excitable personality, inconstancy, irritability, a tendency to cause unrest to others.

Mars semi-square AS: a fighting spirit, forcing one's will on others, to lead others resolutely, to be actively creative in team-work.

Mars = Moon/Neptune: Hypersensitivity, weakened procreative powers.

AS = Moon/Neptune: licentiousness, dependence on influences from the environment, the ability to see through others.

AS = Neptune/MC: living in a world of phantasy, play acting.

Here we have several configurations which at first sight do not seem to correlate with Goethe's personality. Following Saturn conj. AS could Goethe be described as an inhibited man? Here we may recall that Goethe was apparently dead when born and probably only came to life when the ascendant had passed from Saturn to the square of Uranus (sudden awakening). While later in life

Goethe often felt not only inhibited but also shut in and that this unfoldment was being curtailed. When in Weimar he had to carry out his duties as a civil servant and was therefore unable to devote himself entirely to his poetry. On several occasions he even felt obliged to escape from his environment. Likewise the highly sensitive, unbalanced characteristics noted can be correlated to the nature of the poet. One calls to mind here “Leiden des jungen Werther” (“The suffering of young Werther”). In a letter Goethe writes: (26)

“In the sufferings of young Werther I portray a young man who with pure and deep sensitivity and gifted with penetrating powers loses himself in romantic dreams, succumbing to fanciful speculation, until finally with the additional burden of unhappy passions, his eternal love destroyed, he puts a gun to his temple and pulls the trigger.”

When Goethe wrote this work he was himself in the condition he describes. He freed himself by writing his “sufferings” out of his soul.

Summing up the cosmic conditions of his Ascendant:

At times the environment causes inhibitions so that the personality is unable to unfold according to his own free will. However his own will will always reassert itself overcoming these inhibitions and the tendency to unsteadiness. At times the personality will withdraw into a world of make-believe, the true ego hiding under an outer mask. This for Goethe was the world of the theatre and art in general.

It is probably safe to assume in the chart of a philosopher and poet that Mercury will occupy a significant position. From Mercury’s structural picture we see that it is square to Pluto and in the midpoints Moon/Uranus, Moon/AS, Mars/Neptune. Referring to CSI we find the following interpretations:

Mercury square Pluto: the art of persuasion, suggestion, restless thinking, good powers of observation, quick grasp of every situation, amazingly sharp criticism, intellectual victory over others, cunning, craftiness, diplomacy, contradictory spirit, irritability, overestimation of self. A convincing speaker, the ability to influence the masses, a critic, a writer.

Mercury = Moon/Uranus: intuition, good ideas, suggestive train of thought, intellectually alert and lively.

Pluto = Moon/Uranus: self-willedness, stubbornness, fanaticism, a craving for sensation.

Pluto = Moon/AS: disharmonious relationships with females in the environment, personal relationships with tragic consequences.

Mercury = Moon/AS: adaptability, sociableness, to cultivate the exchange of ideas and thoughts, changing relationships.

Mercury = Mars/Neptune: thoughtlessness, nervous weakness (in consequence of misuse of one's creative energies and drugs) weakness of mind, sensitive nerves (receptive mind).

Pluto = Mars/Neptune: causing or receiving violent Injury (dissolution, death). (We shall see later that this configuration was in evidence at the time of Goethe's death).

With reference to Pluto's position in a cosmogram it has to be pointed out that Pluto can only have personal significance when it is in aspect with other planets and the personal points. For the slow moving planets—and to date Pluto is still the slowest—are as far as their general position is concerned characteristic of a whole generation. In Goethe's time thinking on cosmopolitan lines was in vogue. With this came the French Revolution. When therefore, as here, we find Mercury square Pluto we may legitimately deduce that the analysis, discussion and taking of sides on the issues of the day would not be exclusive to the realms of politics but would also be felt in the "Sturm und Drangperiode" (Revolutionary Period) of the new young generation of artists. (That the French Revolution made a deep impression on Goethe, and that he had to come to grips with it can be seen in his cosmogram. Transiting Pluto was conjunction his radical Uranus at that time.)

A summary of the cosmic conditions of Goethe's Mercury might read as follows:

Through restless thinking, good powers of observation, a quick grasp of every situation, a personal critical viewpoint, intuition and a wealth of ideas, it is possible to influence many people through speech or the written word, and to stimulate a lively exchange of thought and prepare the way for social contacts. Irritability, impatience, stubbornness and an overestimation of self-will also show themselves on occasions.

The positions of Venus and Jupiter in Goethe's cosmogram are very interesting. CSI gives the following interpretations for these positions:

Venus opposition Jupiter: a warm heart, grace, tact, attractive personality, to be able to make oneself popular, harmonious relationship with other people, excellent sense of form or shape, love of ease, negligence, incorrect conduct in love, wastefulness, intense inner life, excessive expression of feelings. Artists.

Venus sextile Neptune: sensitive in love, easily influenced, receptive to beauty, art and music, dreamy nature, good taste, high ideals, mistaken sense of love, seducible character, amorous aberrations. Artists.

Venus = Sun/Node: interested in artistic performance, to seek associations with artists or people interested in art.

Jupiter = Sun/Node: The desire to gain recognition in public life, generosity, tact, sociableness, harmonious integration into the community.

Saturn = Sun/Node: lack of adaptability, reserve, inhibitions with regard to other people.

Venus semi-square Saturn: sense of reality, sobriety, a sense of duty, economy, reserve, loyalty, self-control, emotional inhibitions, being unsatisfied in love, unhealthy expression of the sex-urge, self-tormenting jealousy.

Venus = Node/MC: the desire to reveal one's innermost feelings and inclinations in personal associations, to be able to love with one's whole heart.

Jupiter = Node/MC: a love of jolly sociability, a liking for convivial social get-to-gethers in comfort, a happy inner understanding with others (Frau v. Stein!)

Saturn = Node/MC; to prefer to go one's own way, to be withdrawn, egotistic, to seclude oneself from others.

Venus = Mercury/Neptune: rapturous imagination, over-expectations in love, strong powers of attraction of short duration. a strong fluid-like emanation.

Jupiter = Mercury/Neptune: rich imagination, fanciful perceptions, enhanced powers of imagination. Poet, Actor.

Saturn = Mercury/Neptune: muddled picturing and perceiving, pessimistic outlook, inhibitions in thinking, egotistic imagination, morbid sensitivity.

We can see from this summary that we have here an art lover, an artist or poet, who can become popular and gain public recognition. At times he will be very romantic in love but then comes down to earth again, so that any mutual attraction is usually only of short duration.

We should not expect to find genius confirmed in CSI. Such a diagnosis exceeds the framework of cosmic factors.

Do not be put off by several apparent inconsistencies. Life is often very changeable. For each experience.one will find the cosmic correlations. Thus an experience or attitude which does not manifest until late in life is still depicted in the cosmogram but it will not materialize until the configurations of the day or the directions activate it.

It would take up too much space and probably bore the reader to deal with every single factor in Goethe's chart in a similar way but the method of investigation should be clear from the example given.

Some readers may perhaps feel that the signs of the zodiac have not been considered sufficiently here. Reference to these can be looked up in CSI as well as in *Kosmopsychologie* (27) and elsewhere. But this aside experience has shown that the essential aptitudes and qualities of an individual can be grasped sufficiently solely from a consideration of the mutual inter-relationships of the planets, Sun, Moon, MC and Moon's Node.

Solar Arc Directions

When the cosmogram has been computed and the most important points interpreted, the question arises:

When will these various configurations manifest themselves?

Two possibilities present themselves:

1. Stimulation by directions: (28) the direction of the individual positions in the cosmogram by one of the various methods in use.
2. Stimulation by transits: the passage of the actual day to day planets over the various sensitive points in the birth chart.

A later chapter will be devoted to the matter of transits. Here we will consider the question of directions. There are various methods in use:

The one-degree method (OD), by which all factors in the chart are advanced by one degree for each year of life. Naibod's Measure where the factors are not advanced by one degree for each year of life but instead according to the Sun's mean daily motion. Solar Arc directions are based on the theory that:

1 day's motion of the Sun = 1 year of life

How is the solar arc calculated?

To calculate the solar arc for one day subtract the position of the Sun in the ephemeris for one day from the position of the Sun on the following day. If we wish to calculate the solar arc for the 22nd year of life in Goethe's chart we add 22 days to his birthday, the 28 August, giving us the 50th subtracting the 31 days of August gives us the 19th September. Now to compute the Sun's motion for this interval we can use an ephemeris for any year as the variation in the Sun's motion for any given date varies only very slightly from year to year.

Here according to our ephemeris:

Sun's position on 19 September	22°04'16" Virgo
Sun's position on 28 August	4°41'41" Virgo
Thus the solar arc for age 22 years is:	21°22'35"

(The calculation of solar arc directions will be greatly facilitated by the use of the *booklet Table of Events* (29). This is so arranged that only a small calculation is needed to determine the solar arc for any year.)

The 90°-dial can be used to great effect when working with these directions.

Our K2 chart form has two large circles around which are marked the 90° divisions. For the investigation of the birth chart itself we cut out the smaller circle. For calculating the directions a second form is used and the larger circle is cut out. This is then placed exactly concentrically beneath the smaller circle. Great care should be taken here to ensure that the two zero points coincide exactly. This done now transcribe the positions of the factors on the smaller inner circle on to the larger outer circle. When this has been done loosen the central nut a little and move the zero, 0° Aries, point of the outer 90° circle by the amount corresponding to the solar arc for the year of life under consideration. In this simple way it is possible to examine the configurations of each year of life.

At 22, Goethe had his first serious love affair with Fredericke von Sesenheim. As this acquaintance began a few months before his birthday in 1771 (according to some, as early as October 1770) we will work with an approximate solar arc of 21° Therefore the zero point on the outer circle is now rotated to coincide with the 21° marking on the inner circle as in Fig. 13. Now let us investigate the relationships of the directed planets, identified by an "s", with

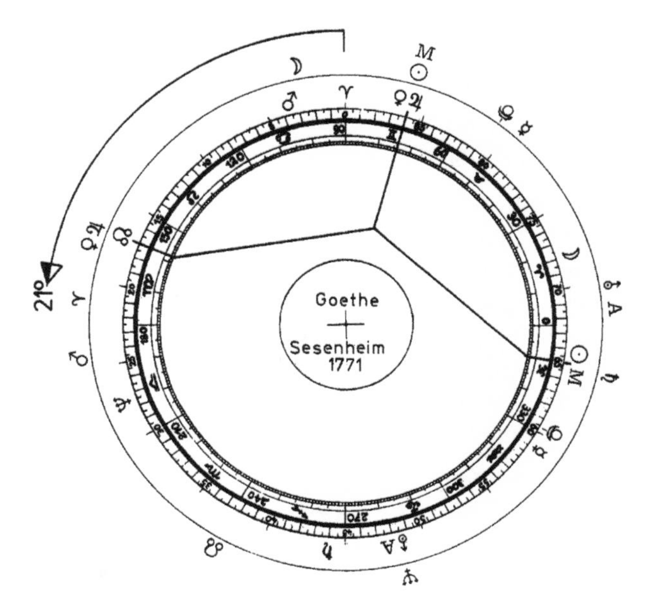

Fig. 13 Goethe's episode in Sesenheim. Inner circle: radical chart; outer circle: planets around the solar arc of 21° s.

the positions in the radical chart, identified by an "r".

(At one time we used the letter "v to signify the progressed planets. However this had little meaning outside of Germany. For this reason we have substituted the internationally accepted letter "s" to signify directions by solar arc. This might sometimes give rise to confusion as it could also stand for solar chart, though we do not ourselves use this method in our work.)

Examining the inner and outer positions we find to our surprise that we are able to establish certain facts at a glance. At the top of the chart MC s and Sun s are seen to be conjunct Venus r and Jupiter r. Slightly to the left Moon s is with Mars r, whilst to the far left we find Venus s and Jupiter s are with Node r. At the bottom right Neptune s is with Uranus r and middle right Saturn s is with Sun rand MC r. Calculating the exact positions for these we have:

MC s 26°	= ☉ s 26°09'	= ♀ r 26°244'	= ♃ r 26°00
	☽ s 3°00'	= ♂ r 3°28'	
♀ s 27°24'	♃ s 17°00'	= ☊ r 17o00'	
	♆ s 18°30'	= ♅ r 18o33'	
	♄ s 4°45'	= ☉ r 5°09'	= MCr 5°00

Now it will be seen that these directed factors given here cannot be considered in isolation. For just as these factors stand in certain mid-points in the radical chart so equally these directed factors will continue to stand in the same relationship with the directed mid-points. In the example above it should be noted that we have a special type of case wherein the directed factors coincide with elements which were already present in their radical midpoint configurations. Consider the following picture:

♀ ♃. . . . . ☉	M	s. . . . .♄ s
☊ r. . . . . ♀	♃	r. . . . .☉ MC r
Happy love affair	happy and deep affection	to withdraw to feel sad

Goethe enjoyed very happy times with Fredericke. However he also felt himself pulled in two directions by the relationship, between: "The bliss of being loved" and the doubt the "I do not know whether I love you. " For the first time he experienced a sense of guilt from which he tried to free himself through his poetry, bestowing immortality on Fredericke in the process.

From this example we can see how the radical tendencies (Sun = MC = Venus/Saturn: being dissatisfied, reserved) are combined by direction with the Venus = Jupiter = Saturn in mid-points which juxtapose romantic imagination, strong attraction of short duration, incorrect behavior in love, and emotional reserve. This complex interplay of different mid-points and aspects can hardly be grasped without the use of the 90°-dial.

Goethe's meeting with the Duke Carl August von Weimar and his subsequent move to Weimar mark the commencement of a very significant period in goethe's life. He arrived in Weimar on the 7th November 1775. He was then 26 years 2 months old. To find the solar arc for this time we refer to the *Tables of Events* already mentioned (29).

With these tables it is not necessary to calculate the solar arc for each particular event separately. Instead we can look up the mean solar arc for 45 years which is given for each day of the year in Table III calculated by Helmut Ahner.

Using this arc as given we can then enter Table II under the appropriate column and read off the mean solar arc for the age under investigation. Thus here turning to Table III for the 28th August, Goethe's birthday, we find that the mean solar arc for 45 years is given as 44°00'19".

Referring to Table II under the various arcs for 45 years given at the bottom of each column we find one for 44°00'00".

Taking our first example we find the mean arc for age 22 years is 21°30'40". This is 8' more than the value calculated above due to the fact that we are dealing with mean values. It will be seen that these are convenient and sufficiently accurate for general surveys.

When more precise values for the solar arc are required these can be calculated in the usual manner from Table I which gives the position of the Sun for each day of the year. In the present example, for age 26, Table II gives a mean arc of 25°25'20". Calculating the exact solar arc for September 1775 when the first meeting seems to have taken place, we obtain a value of 25°18' which for precision will be used here.

Turning to our 90°-dial we now rotate the 0°Aries point on the large outer chart so that it coincides with 25°181 on the smaller inner chart as shown in Fig. 14. It is not difficult to spot immediately the important combinations for this event: directed Pluto contacting radical Jupiter.

According to CSI Jupiter-Pluto contacts mean to achieve leadership. It was indeed unusual for a young man of 26 to become an advisor to a ruler and to rise to first minister of his country.

Now to enlarge the basic picture in this example we can examine the mid-points which gives us the following:

☽ s. . . . . ☉ ☿ s. . . . . ♅ s

17°18' : 24°38'

☽/♅ s

25°34'

☊ r. . . . . ♃ r. . . . . ☉ MCr

17°00' 26°00' 5°00'

MC/☊ r

11°04'/26°04'

When writing down the individual positions as here it is probably best to enter the degrees and minutes so as to be able to compare them but to omit the signs.

We have already seen that the above Mercury-Pluto combination is of great importance for thinking and particularly for poetic activity, as it predisposes to a creative shaping and planning of ideas. These qualities may manifest themselves equally in a statesman who must needs be circumspect, far-sighted, purposeful and able to organize, lead, etc.

Here Pluto, its cosmic conditions interpreted in this sense, activates the radical Jupiter. Directed Pluto is at 26°Sagittarius and forms a square to Jupiter. As was pointed out earlier it would seem that important events in a life are nearly always released by conjunctions, and the squares and oppositions, those aspects in fact considered unfavourable in traditional astrology.

This Pluto-complex not only releases Jupiter but also the radical Venus, Sun/Node and Node/MC. It follows therefore that this turn of events is likely to be decisive in respect also to love and art.

It was in fact not until Weimar that Goethe had the opportunity to meet the great thinkers of his time, and notably Schiller. Here Venus = Sun/Node is characteristic of associations with artists and friends of the arts. Venus = Node/MC allows for the development of personal affections and wholehearted love. Jupiter = Sun/Node signifies recognition in public life, sociability, and points to a harmonious integration into the community—in this case into society

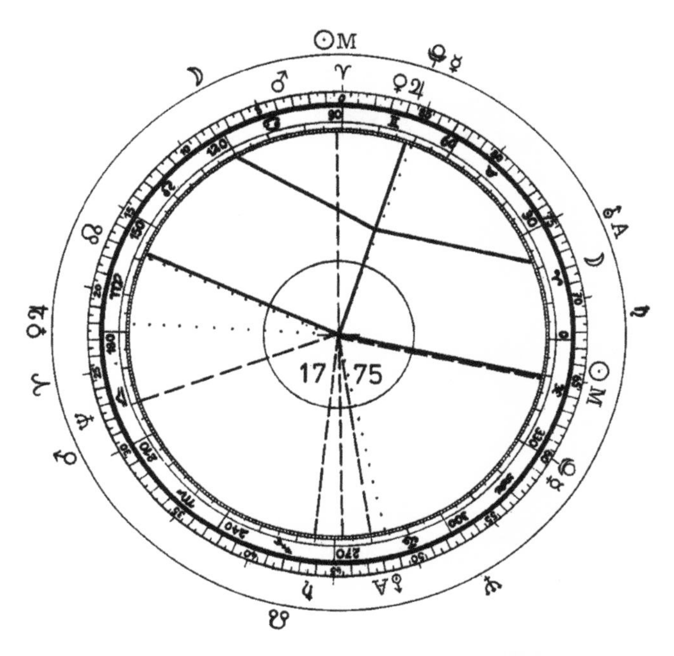

Fig. 14 Meeting with the Duke Carl August; move to Weimar; inner circle: radical chart; outer circle: planets around the solar arc 25°18' s

as well as into the world of statesmanship. Jupiter = Node/MC points to the soul union that developed with Charlotte von Stein. Pluto = Sun/Node and Pluto = Node/ MC signify the desire to "influence the masses", that is to influence a wider sphere beyond the immediate environment. Pluto contacts give perseverance, the right choice of collaborators, organising ability and finally lead to great achievements. All the above interpretations have been put together directly from CSI and in no way rest on arbitrary speculation.

Up to now we have been discussing only those combinations that instantly leap to the eye, those which result from the immediate alignment of directed factors with radical ones. But we can also investigate each directed factor and its relationship to the radical planets and mid-points and vice versa.

It is best to proceed with these investigations systematically. First place the indicator of the dial to 0°Aries on the inner chart. Moving the indicator to the left we first come to the directed positions of the Sun and MC. We see at once that the Sun s and MC s have just passed the radical axes Mars/Jupiter and Venus/Mars:

Sun s
0°27'
MC s
0°18'

Mars r .... 26°24' Venus r
3°28' Jupiter r
26°00'

Venus/Mars
14°56'/29°56'
Mars/Jupiter
14°44'/29°44'

In the case of the above mid-points two positions are given: the direct and the indirect. The indirect position is the angle of 45° to the mid-point which is the one which in this case corresponds numerically with the directed positions. Sun s is at 0°27' (or 30°27') and here the relationship to Venus/Mars at 29°56' is easier to see than if this position were given as 14°56'. The author's assumption that the 45° and 135° aspects are of equal strength to other angular aspects has been confirmed statistically by Dr. Theodor Landscheidt (30). Therefore it is not absolutely necessary to indicate the angle of aspect each time. It should be sufficient to know that one factor has a relationship with another. Here it would also be correct to write: Sun s : Venus/Mars

In other words the Sun by solar arc is in aspect to the midpoint Venus/Mars. However the use of the equation sign in such formulae has been so universally accepted that it would be difficult to discard it now. Of course it is in fact completely correct when considered in relation to the 90°-circle. Here the Sun s is 0°27' = Venus 86°24' + Mars 3°28' = 89°52' : 2 = 44°56'. Therefore the Sun s and the mid-point Venus/Mars in 44°56' are almost exactly opposite one another so that they form an axis halving the 90°-circle.

What does Sun s = Venus/Mars signify? Physical love, the urge to union between man and woman. MC = Venus/Mars is individual indulgence in sensuality, the urge to become one with the other in soul and body, sexual relationships. At the same time Sun s = Mars/Jupiter, which may indicate an engagement, as also might MC s = Mars/Jupiter. If we check in a biography of goethe's life we find that in January 1775 he had a close relationship with Lili Schonemann and became engaged three months later.

"We can see what a dangerous blonde this was. Not a flower in the woods like her, not one flowering in the window of a quiet house like Lotte, but unfolding in the center of a magnificent garden between fountains admired by everyone. " It was a "growing passion, his happiness, and then the awakening from this ecstasy."

Moving, the outer chart forward by half a degree we can see the situation after the engagement. A whole new turn of events: the call to Weimar which in the first place entailed disappointments and separations.

The picture that emerges is:

Sun s
0°27
MC s
0°18'

Sun r

Neptune r. . . . . 5°09'

27°30 16°20'/31°20' MC r

5°00'

Saturn r. . . . . Uranus r

13°45' 31°09 18°33'

15°45'/30°45' AS r

17°45'

This might be interpreted:

Sun s = Sun/Neptune; rich experience in spiritual spheres, mystical experiences, long-distance journeys, success through sympathetic understanding of other people.

For the configuration Sun = Sun/Neptune, in which one link of the mid-point is part of the mid-point itself, no separate interpretation is given in CSI. Such a combination may be interpreted as a reinforcement of the basic meaning of the mid-point Sun/Neptune, but tending towards the triggering factor of the mid-point, in this case the Sun. Here looking at the Sun as positive and Neptune as negative, since it is the positive tendencies that are being stressed these are the more likely to be released in this case. This is confirmed by the facts of Goethe's taking a long-distance journey and the "sympathetic understanding" of other people involved.

MC s = Sun/Neptune: individual sensitivity, being weak or easily influenced, a negative attitude. (The dissolution of the relationship with Lili Schonemann).

MC s = Neptune/MC: devotion to peculiar objectives, inclination to feign, pose or put on an act. (?)

Sun s = Saturn/Uranus: separation (from Frankfurt, from his habitual relationships. Grimm says of this that Goethe's move from Frankfurt to Weimar would at that time have been a greater transition than for example moving to America from Europe today.)

MC s = Saturn/Uranus: separation

Sun s = Saturn/AS: an awareness of lack of freedom of movement, the desire to go one's own way, difficult circumstances of living, sufferings from the conditions imposed by the environment, becoming ill, separation.

MC s = Saturn/AS: soul suffering through separation, to be hindered in the fulfillment of one's objectives in life. (These hampering influences were now being lifted.)

Now moving the indicator of the dial on the next factor, the Moon, we get the following picture:

Moon s
7°18'

Node r. .... Venus 26°24'
17°00'   21°42'/6°42'   Jupiter
21°30'/6°30'   26°00'
Saturn r. .... Pluto
13°45'   22°01'/7°01'   0°18'
6°23'   Mercury
Neptune s
22°48'/7°48'

Considering the above mid-points we see that the Moon has already passed over Venus/Node and Jupiter/Node. The love relationship with a women is therefore already past. But the separation combinations are still operative:

Moon s = Saturn/Pluto: tragic destiny of a women (separation from Lili)
Neptune s = Saturn/Pluto: shattered nerves (perhaps being a young man this did not happen, and as such we might translate this as suffering through separation, for the bond with Lili continued to be felt by Goethe for many years.)
Moon s = Mercury/Saturn: separation from a woman.
Neptune s = Mercury/Saturn: Longing for faraway places, an unnecessary (?) journey.

It can be seen from this picture that the Moon signifies both the feelings and connections with females. It indicates the past love affair as well as the separation.

Again Venus and Jupiter play a prominent part. And here we need to get away from the concept that Venus always relates to love. Venus also corresponds to art, beauty, the muse of inspiration.

Venus s
21°42’
Jupiter s
21°18’

Neptune.		. . . . .Node
27°30’	22°15’	17°00’
Uranus.		. . . . .Venus
18°33’	7°28’/22°28’	26°40’
Uranus		Jupiter
18°33’	7°28’/22°28’	26°40’
AS.		. . . . Venus
17°45’	7°04’/22°04’	26°40’
AS		Jupiter
17°45’	6°52’/21°52’	26°00’
Mercury.		. . . . Moon
29°02’	5°31’/20°31’	12°00’
Pluto		Moon
0°18’	6°09’/21°09’	12°00’

Venus s = Neptune/Node: wrong connections, unfaithfulness (Parting from Lili).

Jupiter s = Neptune/Node: experiencing disappointments, placing great hopes upon new associations (Duke Carl August).

Venus s = Venus/Uranus: love adventure, unfaithfulness (Lili).

Jupiter s = Venus/Uranus: sudden and passing happiness in love (Lili), artistic success (Goethe’s artistic success laid the foundation for his connection with Weimar).

Venus s = Jupiter/Uranus: changing live relationship, artistic acknowledgment.

Jupiter s = Jupiter/Uranus: fortunate turn of luck in life, a sudden turn of destiny, sudden recognition, successful speculation.

Venus s = Moon/Mercury: young love (This configuration would have been exact a year or so before thus relating to Lili).

Jupiter s = Moon/Mercury: a happy young woman (This position is over by this time).

Venus s = Moon/Pluto: intense stepping up of love feelings (now past).

Jupiter s = Moon/Pluto: great success, lucky chances (also past).

Setting the dial to directed Mars we find that the aspects to Neptune are now over but that the following planetary pictures are still current:

	Mars s 28°46’	
Mercury 29°02’	27°43’/2°43’	Venus 26°24’
Mercury 29°02’	27°31’/12°31’	Jupiter 26°00’
Pluto 0°18’	28°41’/13°41’	Venus 26°40’
Pluto 0°18	28°09’/13°09’	Jupiter 26°00’
	Uranus s 28°51’/13°51’	
	AS s 28°03’/13o03’	

While the mid-points at the top of this axis have been operative for some time and may be seen to relate to Goethe’s last love experience, the mid-points at the bottom of this axis indicate the very favourable influences operating at this turn of events in his life:

Mars s = Jupiter/Pluto: organising talent, the ability to inspire others with enthusiasm, the desire to achieve great things.
Uranus s = Jupiter/Pluto: sudden reform, quick development, adjustment to new circumstances.
AS s = Jupiter/Pluto: prudence, far-sightedness, organizing talent, the desire for power, personal advancement.
Mars s = Venus/Pluto: an unusual experience in love.
AS s = Venus/Pluto: an attractive personality wielding a great influence upon other people, an unusual introduction to a loved person.

These latter configurations might refer to Goethe’s relationship with Charlotte von Stein. Though of course the involvement of

Venus/Pluto here would reveal this association in a somewhat different light to that generally presented. But it must have been an unusually deep affection. Although this love has been alluded to repeatedly in Goethe's poems, almost all the letters of Charlotte von Stein to Goethe have been destroyed.

Setting the dial to the directed Node we see that the contact with the Venus/Jupiter axis is already past. Neptune s has already been discussed in connection with the Moon s. The directed Saturn configured with the mid-points Sun/Moon and Moon/MC (dissolution of a physical and soul union) would seem to have already had their effect.

Now just as we can examine the interaction of the directed factors with the mid-points in the radical chart, so too we can examine the relationship of the radical positions to the directed mid-points.

Thus here we find:

Mars r
3°28'
MC s
Moon s. . . . . 5°00'
3°48'
Sun s
5°09'
AS
7°45'/2°45'
Uranus
18°33'/3°33'

How are these directed mid-points calculated?

The radical Moon/MC mid-point lies in 17° : 2 = 8°30'. The solar arc for the move to Weimar is 25°18'. Adding this to the radical mid-point, 8°30' + 25°18' we get the total of 33°48' or 3°48'. From CSI we find that the meaning of the Sun and Moon is not limited to the relationship of man (Sun) and woman (Moon). In this particular case the following interpretation would seem more appropriate:

Mars r = Sun/Moons: desire to realise ideals and wishes, the realisation of joint objectives.

AS r = Sun/Moon s: frank and open behaviour towards other people, the desire to make new contacts and acquaintances.

Uranus r = Sun/Moon s: the urge for freedom, the desire to act independently, a lack of adaptability, inner rebellion, separation of partners.

Mars r = Moon/MC s: the devotion of body and soul to a task, to act through soul motives, industriousness, ambition, the desire to possess a woman's soul (This position does not become exact until a few months later and would appear to refer to Charlotte von Stein).

AS r = Moon/MC s: an emotional attitude to one's environment, the understanding of other people spiritually.

Uranus r = Moon/MC s: an unusual degree of emotional excitability (caused by the change from Frankfurt to Weimar).

If we want to calculate when a particular solar arc direction becomes exact we proceed as follows: since c. 60' = 12 months, then c. 5' = 1 month. A difference of 20' would therefore correspond to four months. In a letter to Johanna Fahlmer of February 14, 1776, Goethe writes among other things: "A magnificent soul is this Frau von Stein, to whom one might say I am attached and with whom I have nestled down." This contact must therefore have been made by the middle of February.

Further aspects between the radical and directed factors be summarised briefly here:

Saturn r = Sun/Pluto s: ruthless overcoming of obstacles and difficulties, separation.

Saturn r = Pluto/MC s: self-sacrifice, attaining one's objectives through sacrifice, toilsome struggle of existence (As a servant of the Duke's, Goethe was obliged to give up some personal freedom, especially in the early days).

Mercury r = Node/AS s: to seek and receive mental stimuli, research and study together with other people.

Mercury r = Uranus/Node s: quick comprehension, to be united in thought with others, sudden understanding with others, to criticise others.

Pluto r = Uranus/Node s: the desire to influence other people or to be influenced oneself, exciting or upsetting experiences shared with other people (Goethe was placed in the company of an arrogant nobility used to its own ways and he had to hold his own sometimes under "exciting" circumstances).

Pluto r = Sun/Mars s: fanaticism or partiality, the desire to achieve a lot, ruthless procedure (ruthless rupture of old connections).

Pluto r = Mars/MC s: extraordinary aspirations and great vigor. the desire to accomplish immense tasks.

Sun r = Pluto/Node s: the desire to impose one's will upon others or vice versa.

MC r = Pluto/Node s: fate dependent upon associations and contacts with others, associations influence the objectives in life and somehow cause set backs to the career. (This interpretation is undoubtedly confirmed by facts).

Moon r = Saturn/AS s: separations from females (the breaking of the engagement to Lili).

Jupiter r = Pluto s: this has already been dealt with under Pluto s = Jupiter r

This survey shows how with the aid of the 90°-dial the complex configurations in a cosmogram can be worked- out, and correspondence found between the cosmic factors calculated and the actual facts. The reader should really get a detailed biography of Goethe (obtainable from any library) and underline all those interpretations that are confirmed in the course of his life.

Under no circumstances should one lose oneself in a maze of details but always endeavor to comprehend the situation as a whole, as is possible with these relatively simple methods. It will soon be appreciated that a great deal of what is known as traditional astrology may be dispensed with.

Here we have computed our examples exactly in order to bring out the possible precision. But in general computing should always take second place to visual recognition. In this way one will quickly grasp the interdependent relationships visually and the dial will only be needed for purposes of checking. Nor should one worry unduly about minutes. There are those specialists who like to calculate configurations to the minute, seeking to foretell events to the day if possible, or even to the hour. That is of course very commendable and not unimportant in research. However we should always keep in mind that whilst it is possible to compute the cosmic factors precisely for a given time, in most cases the actual conditions in which the person happens to be placed are not likely to be known so precisely.

When attempting forecasts one can never be too careful. The more one goes into detail the more likely are disappointments. Anyone who wishes to gain experience by investigating past events and their correlating configurations would remember only to include those points which could have been used for making a forecast.

Here the solar arc directions are of great value. With the aid of the 90°-dial these can be quickly and simply applied for the year of life under consideration and nearly always prove effective.

Another advantage of the solar arc directions is that any ephemeris may be used for their calculation (or the *Table of Events*) and therefore one does not need to obtain other ephemerides.

In certain circumstances one may not wish to go to the trouble of examining all the configurations but may wish only to investigate certain factors correlating to special objectives or events. Staying with our example chart we may ask whether the event of Goethe's death can perhaps be seen with the aid of the 90°-dial.

Here we must differentiate between those forecasts made before an event takes place and retrospective investigation of events that have already occurred. One should never take it upon oneself to forecast death. It is only very rarely possible, because other factors which cannot be known from the cosmic conditions alone will all have their influence.

When we examine Mercury and Pluto in the birth chart (p. 43) we noted the combination: Pluto = Mars/Neptune: causing or receiving brutal damage (dissolution, death).

We have already pointed out that this combination was in evidence at the time of Goethe's death. If we set the outer dial to the solar arc direction for the year of death, 81°27', and place the indicator on Pluto we see that this point coincides with the directed Mars/Saturn mid-point in 0°03' (Pisces) Pluto being in 0°18' Sagittarius. Therefore we have here:

Pluto r = Mars/Saturn s: force majeure
Pluto r = Mars/Neptune r: dissolution, death

The correlation is clear. But we should not conclude from this that this planetary configuration caused death. This would be totally wrong. A more likely interpretation would be that the native had reached the age of 83 when death might be expected.

It is however significant that death does seem to correlate with definite cosmic rhythms. At the time of Goethe's death transiting Neptune was in 27° Capricorn which means that it had covered exactly half of the zodiac between his birth and death. At birth Neptune was posited in the mid-point Mars/Uranus, which indicates a certain weakness. At birth the baby had to be awakened to life. Here at death the same configuration indicated senility.

Uranus was in 17° Aquarius at the time of death having just completed one cycle of the zodiac during the life time.

This example shows that other cosmic rhythms are operative in addition to the solar arc directions. It is therefore recommended that a variety of methods should be used as a check.

A Prediction Is Wrong

The best examples are not always those in which everything is confirmed and all is proved right, in Which one confirmation follows on another. It has been repeatedly pointed out that it would be impossible for all forecasts to be correct since the cosmic factor is only one of several. We would combine the prediction of possible developments with the wish to counter these cosmic influences by applying our will and thus be able to avert any danger or crisis indicated.

On the other hand, one does want to make full use of the favorable configurations. This of course does not mean that with a foreknowledge of coming favorable positions we may draw the big prize in the lottery or become millionaires overnight. Whoever cherishes such hopes will soon be terribly disappointed. Configurations which have up to now been considered favorable do not at times appear to work out.

Various specialists—astrologers really to be taken seriously—have investigated the following case, without coming to any satisfactory conclusion. Again and again favorable positions were computed, configurations that promised the overcoming of a crisis. Yet each time the woman answered that her tormenting times were not over and that no turning point had been reached. We will trace the origin of these mistakes after we have thoroughly studied the cosmogram.

We are dealing with a female born on 28th September, 1901, at 3:30 a.m. 47°33'N and 7°40'E (Fig. 15). The small drawing corresponds to the traditional presentation with the Ascendant being

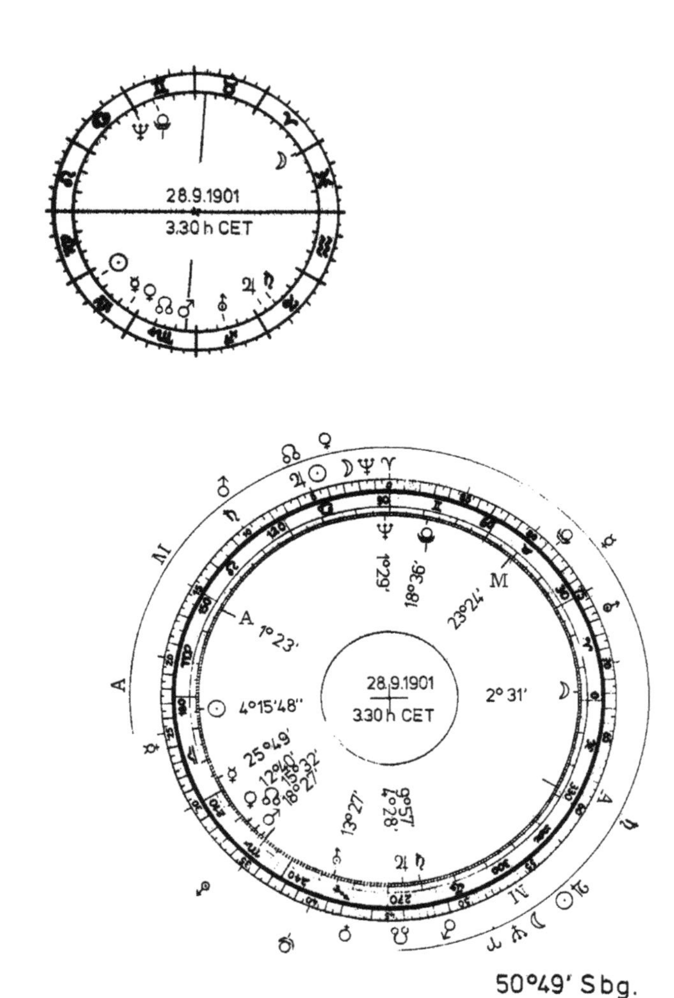

Fig. 15 A prediction is wrong. The smaller figure shows the horizon horizontally. When using the combined chart it is recommended always to place 0°Cancer and 0 of the 90°-circle at the top, this means of course that the AS and the MC will take up different positions.

horizontal. You will note that nearly all the planets are in the lower part of the cosmogram, so that according to tradition, we have here a largely introverted personality who receives and digests impressions from the environment, but is herself unable to give out or actively influence her environment to any extent. Life as such is taken somewhat seriously.

Apart from this, the birth chart shows a grand cross, which is formed by the Sun, Moon, Jupiter and Neptune. From this alone we are able to conclude that there will be no lack of conflicts in life.

Venus and Mars are conjunct in Scorpio and connected with grand cross by semi-square and sesquiquadrate.

The lower half of Fig. 15 depicts the cosmogram with the 90°-circle. In this the above mentioned constellations are even more accentuated. Neptune, Moon, Sun and Jupiter are within 3° exactly opposite Mars. The Neptune axis falls exactly on the Node and Venus/Mars. From this alone we may already deduce that—carefully expressed—no real satisfaction is likely to be attained in love and marriage. But again we will proceed systematically and apply our calculating dial to the individual factors one by one. According to CSI we get the following interpretations:

Sun square Jupiter: health, success, recognition

This Jupiter-Sun contact would have to be taken as positive, if the cosmic condition of the Sun and Jupiter could otherwise be called positive. As the following midpoints will show this is not so.

Sun = Saturn/Neptune: physical reaction to emotional suffering, weak vitality, illness.

Jupiter = Saturn/Neptune: easily upset or depressed, sensitivity, narrow-mindedness, egotism.

Mars = Saturn/Neptune: lack of energy, a state of depression, lack of creative power, weak procreative powers.

Sun = Mercury/Uranus: readiness for action, over-zealous character, premature action or hastiness, the ability to grasp a situation quickly.

Jupiter = Mercury/Uranus: quick at repartee, confidence.
Mars = Mercury/Uranus: courage, determination to succeed.
Sun = Node/MC: union based upon physical and emotional factors.
Jupiter = Node/MC: a love of jolly parties and entertainment.
Mars = Node/MC: comradeship.

The position of Sun, Jupiter and Mars in Saturn/Neptune really is a great disadvantage and will be more noticeable at an advanced age than in youth. The other positions, however, will become effective in early years.

The general picture of all the important planetary aspects is shown in the cosmic structure-picture (Fig. 16). We shall single out the most important positions bearing on love and marriage:

Moon square Neptune: sensitivity, the ability to feel and understand other people in a sympathetic manner, touchiness. dissatisfaction, misunderstood.

Of this position we may say that it is often found in the charts of women who feel they are not understood. Those who have the opportunity to investigate the cosmogram of marriage partners who do not understand each other and part again, will find this Moon-Neptune contact in many divorced wives' charts. The Moon moves swiftly, forming an aspect of 45° to Neptune every 3 or 4 days, therefore, this constellation occurs fairly often.

Moon = Sun/Neptune: dependence of one's feelings or moods on external influences. (The weakening of the functions of the female body).
Neptune = Sun/Jupiter: easily influenced, negative nature, self deception.
Moon = Venus/Mars: strong emotional impulses, an early desire for marriage.
Neptune = Venus/Mars: pathological craving, excesses in love.
Node = Venus/Mars: sensual attraction, sex-union.
Mars = Saturn/Uranus: tensions in love relationships.

The aspect MC sesquiquadrate Saturn is of great importance in

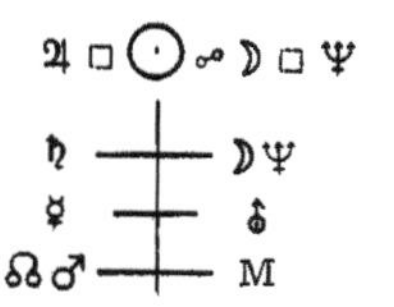

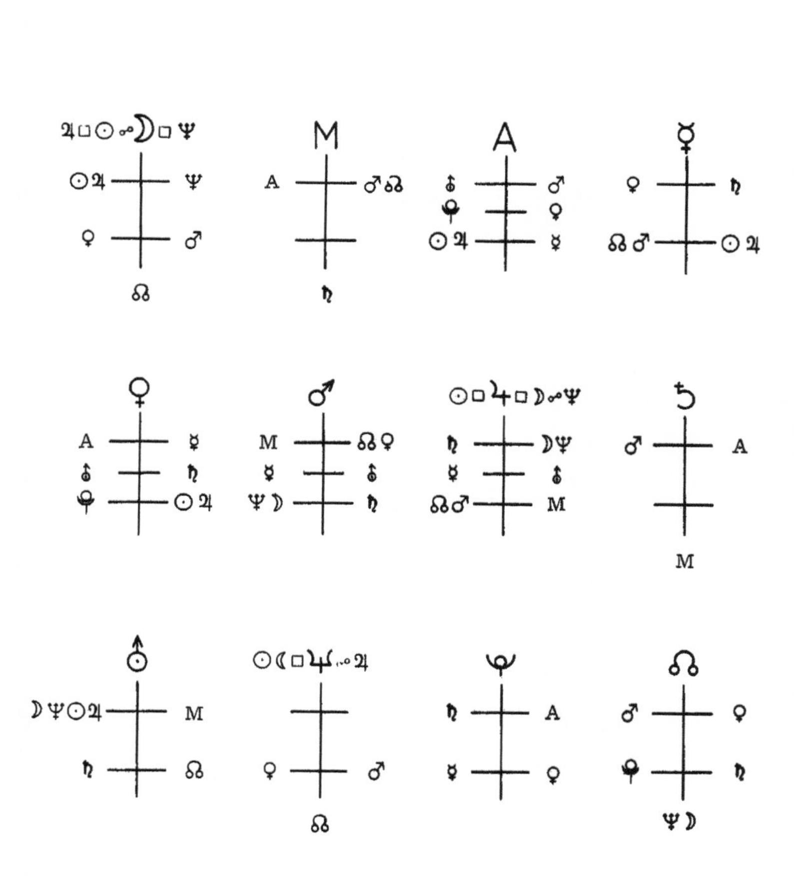

Fig. 16

the overall picture of this chart. If one looks at the 360°-circle at the same time, one will see that here we have MC = Sun/Saturn, giving the following interpretation: inhibitions in the unfoldment of one's own individuality, to exercise reserve, to feel unwell, loneliness, separation.

Summing up the most important points, the indications are of a strongly emotional and passionate disposition (Venus/Mars in Scorpio, Node = Venus/Mars) which may take pathological forms (Neptune = Venus/Mars), a great dependence on moods (Moon = Sun/Neptune) and through disappointment, the contact with a partner may be disturbed time and again.

The weighing up of the contradictory configurations perforce centers on the most prominent positions. An important role is also played by the investigator's own perception and experience. By no means should conclusions be drawn from the cosmic factors alone; the life history, handwriting, photographs, etc. must be taken in to consideration as well, and this presupposes knowledge of psychology and graphology.

From the information obtained we know that this woman married on the 6th July, 1922 and that she gave birth to a son on the 13th January, 1923. who would therefore appear to have been conceived before the wedding. Remember: Moon = Venus/Mars signifying an early desire for marriage. If such dates are available, one should use them for checking purposes. Let us take the wedding day as the critical date. At this time the native was not yet 21 years old. The following computation gives us the solar arc:

28 Sept. 1901 + 21 days = 49 Sept. = 19 Oct. 1901.

Sun on 19 Oct. 1901	= Libra	25°24'22"
Sun on 28 Sept. 1901	= Libra	4°30'06"
Sun-arc for 21 years	=	20°54'16"

Because we are 13 days and two months short of the completion of the 21st year of life, we subtract 10' for two months and 3' for the 13 days, to arrive at the correct solar arc of 20°41' (Fig. 17).

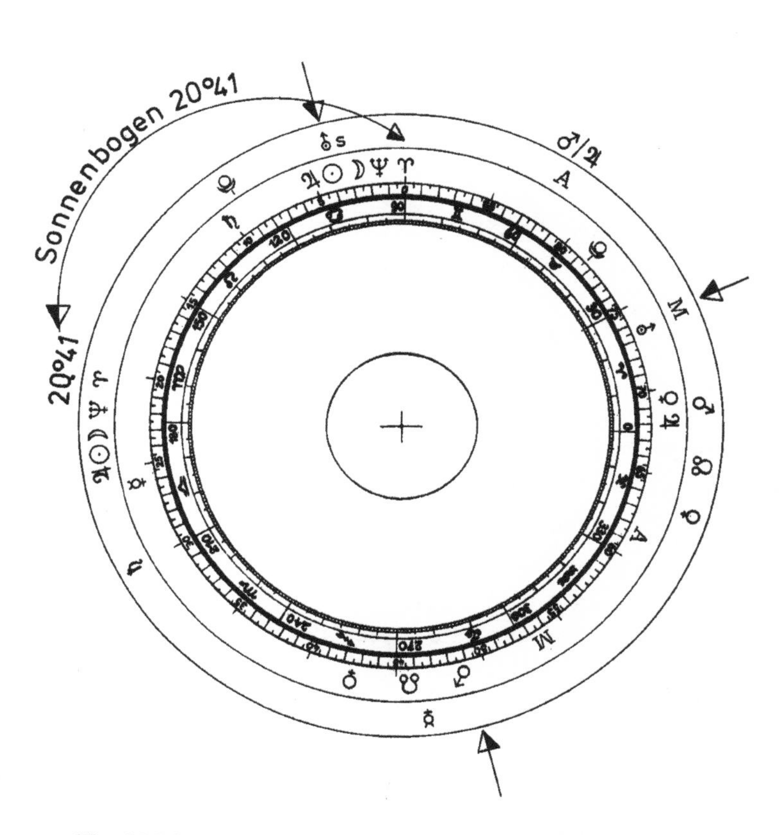

Fig. 17 The outer circle has been advanced by the solar arc for the time of marriage = 20°32'.

The larger outer dial is moved forward so that 0°Aries coincides with 20°41' of the 90°-circle, (the smaller inner one). For preliminary investigations it is more practical to transfer the picture shown by the 90°-dial on to a K2 chart, not only to be able to retain the picture for later use, but also to be able to mark the individual points better. Where correspondences are found, the symbols concerned should be underlined or marked with an arrow.

One will get a few surprises when this cosmogram has been progressed to the wedding day. The following configurations were then current:

Uranus s =	Sun =	Jupiter =	Mars =	Venus/MC
4°08'	4°15'	4°28'	18°27'	18°07'
			3°27'	3°07'

Thence the following interpretation is arrived at:

Venus/MC = Uranus s: deep and sudden inclination.
= Sun r: to be loved.
Venus/MC = Jupiter: to gain affection.
= Mars: sex-union.

Instead of Uranus s = Mars = Jupiter, the following combination may also be taken:

Uranus s = Mars/Jupiter: quick determination, to make a decision suddenly.

In this case, the directed Uranus is not on the midpoint Mars/Jupiter, but rather activates the Mars-Jupiter axis. However, the combination is the same, three planets are in a very definite relationship. The Mars/Jupiter midpoint, or any Mars-Jupiter aspect for that matter, is nearly always involved where an engagement, or a wedding or a birth is concerned.

Furthermore MC s = Uranus is of importance. This combination not only indicates the strength of perseverance to have one's own way, but also a change in life's relationships, when getting married. In the radical chart Uranus is midpoint Jupiter/MC and Sun/MC, therefore correlating to a happy change in life. Since the MC is a participant in these various configurations, it serves to confirm the correctness of this point and the time of birth as well. In addition, Venus s has passed the Ascendant in recent years, corresponding to a love relationship, and this is strengthened by AS on the midpoint Venus/Pluto.

If the indicator of the calculating dial is placed on Mars s, it will be on the midpoints of Venus/Jupiter r and Sun/Venus r, interpreted as: procreation, birth, wedding.

In 1942, the marriage was dissolved, allegedly on the native's initiative. The exact date is not known, but we may use a solar arc of 41°. It has to be assumed that opposite positions to those active on the wedding day will be in force, and this turns out to be the case indeed. Let us move Saturn by 41°; it will then lie at 21° Aquarius or at 51° in the 90°-circle, that is, exactly at the center of Mars/Jupiter, and the interpretation is: to separate. Taking a look at the previous picture, we find Saturn in the complex Sun r = Jupiter r = Mars r, which at the time of marriage was triggered by Uranus s. Saturn s transits Mars, located on the midpoint Ve-nus/MC, in other words, Mars = Venus/MC, pertaining to the sexual relationship, is negated and the ground for a later separation laid. In cases of divorce one must always consider that the actual divorce is the final outcome of a period of mutual difference and difficulties so that the positions of some years past will have to be considered.

Adding 41° to Neptune, it will be at 12°30' Leo, square to Venus. We remember that Venus r = Saturn/Uranus r indicates tensions in the love life leading to separation. Neptune s at this point shows: inability to cope with emotional stresses, and through weakness, acting falsely or malevolently, giving up resistance, separation.

Following these pronouncements let us now look at the year 1952. At this time, the native had approached an astrologer asking him whether her difficulties were now over and when she would again have good prospects regarding love and when an improvement in her financial position might be expected.

For this prognosis the progressed aspects (derived according to the formula: one day after birth corresponding to one year of life) were also utilized but at this point we cannot go into further details. The following aspects were computed and interpreted:

Mars p sextile Mercury r: realization of thoughts and plans.
Node p conjunct Venus: love relationship.
Moon p trine Sun r April 1952; harmonious relationship between a man and a woman.

Uranus t trine Venus: strong impulses, power of attraction. Jupiter t in house X: successes.
Moon s 23°20' Taurus conjunct MC: strong soul-ties.
Saturn s Pisces 0°46' oppositions ASC: estrangement.
Mars s Capricorn 9°16' conjunct Saturn: inhibitions, difficulties.
Venus s Capricorn 3°29' conjunct Jupiter: happiness in love.
Uranus s Aquarius 4°16' trine Sun: sudden turn of events.
Jupiter s Aquarius 25°17' trine Mercury: deeds crowned with success.

The various positions were divided into three groups. Among the progressed aspects we find one sextile and one trine, which according to the author's experience do not have the same power as the so-called hard angles, conjunctions, squares and oppositions. Node progressed conjunct Venus may be considered very powerful, but one will have to take into consideration that the Node moves only about 3' a day (this corresponds to one year of life) so one will have to assume that it is an influence lasting several years.

Jupiter transiting house X means very little, unless he touches important points. Here we remember that MC = Sun/Saturn. Therefore, when Jupiter transits this point, this may indicate a happy separation or contentment in solitude, but not a happy union.

Among the progressed positions, there are some correlating to a soul-union and happiness in love, but others indicate inhibitions, difficulties, estrangement. The most favourable condition to be inferred here is that of happiness in separation in some form or other.

At any rate, the promises made to the native at that time have not been fulfilled. She wrote: "With me everything has remained as it was. I cannot believe that my bad constellations are behind me. You see, six years ago I met and fell in love with a man, but my happiness with him was only brief; he fell in love with and married another woman. Deep inside, I am simply unable to free myself from him. Occasionally I meet him here in this block of flats, and my heart bleeds every time I see him. Don't you see how much I suffer? I would like to move away, but my financial situation is such that I have to remain here. I am without hope and just plain desperate. Every day ideas of suicide cross my mind. . . ."

How does this letter compare with the promising forecasts that were given to this woman from various sources?

Many astrologers may believe and make others believe that the future of a person may be foretold from the stars alone, but by doing so they mislead themselves as well as others. One cannot correctly judge a person's situation or indicate his possibilities of development if one does not also consider the actual circumstances prevailing at the time. In this case we therefore have to take the following considerations into account:

1. From the cosmogram it is seen that the native is very passionate. She became divorced several years ago. Now she lives alone without a man and is in menopause with all its unpleasant side effects.

2. In her enquiry the woman did not mention that she was in love with a married man, that she was pining away longing for him, and would dearly want to have the time calculated when his wife would leave him.

3. In a cosmogram no planet, no position stands on its own; all are part of a whole and can only be considered in relationship to that whole. The pitfalls of all who attempt to make an analysis or prognostication originate from ignorance of this fact. Here the 90°-dial is of great help in grasping the main trends as well as the smallest details in the relationships. To understand all these correctly, one cannot just copy the interpretations from a book of rules; one has to make use of psychology and of one's own experience and knowledge of people.

4. When investigating a cosmogram one must always endeavour to recognise the essence of the chart, and this is generally to be found in the configurations spotted at first glance. These basic positions indicate the nature of and the way the life-force will be used, other relationships among the planets give additional

but less essential information, that nevertheless has its significance.

The most important basic information can be gained by making a structure-picture. Here one will see immediately that the Sun, Moon, Jupiter and Neptune show the strongest mutual relationships, and events in the life have confirmed that these very configurations were triggered by the solar-arc directions.

Naturally the advising astrologer will endeavour not to paint a too gloomy picture of the future, to avoid awakening possible depressive tendencies, but he must also know how far he can go. In this case, it was certainly wrong of the enquirer, when asking for a forecast-analysis, not to mention that she was in love with a married man. Therefore, the investigator had to assume that she was completely free of ties and striving for a second marriage. Correspondingly, the appropriate positions were singled out. Our investigations showed that the picture changed somewhat when the individual factors were not judged by themselves alone, but according to their cosmic condition. Had it been known from the outset that there was a strong feeling of love for a married man and that the native was waiting for the break up of this marriage, then it would have been the duty of the advisor to make the objection-ableness of such an idea clear and to point out the nonsense of those aims, while persuading the native to abandon her hopeless plans. This woman should have been under the care of a psychiatrist.

This example shows how the wrong conclusions may be drawn through not knowing the true circumstances. It has to be stressed again and again that the cosmic factors and their correlations with the lives of human beings can only be judged correctly when the basic information that cannot be seen from the cosmogram, is also given.

The Formation and Dissolution of a Partnership

The situation: An affair which has lasted for 2½ years is coming to an end, apparently because of the silly tittle-tattle of other people. The woman suffers particularly as she is still in love with the man. There is a difference of 16 years in age; however the woman still looks young, as can be seen from a photograph. Up to now, the difference in age has apparently not been noticeable. The question has been asked, is the break permanent or is there still a possibility of coming together again.

Synastry: Figures 18 and 19 depict the birth-charts in the usual presentation. Up to now, in order to be able to determine what contacts there are between the two cosmograms, these would be drawn on transparent paper. The two charts had to be placed on top of each other in such a way that the signs of the zodiac were in identical positions. (Aries on top of Aries, Taurus on top of Taurus etc.) By the traditional method one not only looked for which factors are conjunct, but also for those forming mutual relationships. The 90°-dial facilitates this task considerably.

As we can see from Fig. 20, two 360° and two 90° circles have been used. The letters M and W identify the cosmogram of the man and woman respectively. Of importance are those aspects which coincide most exactly.

Here we have to differentiate between two things. Firstly, the mutual aspects define the interrelationships. They also mark the common points which may be triggered by transits or directions.

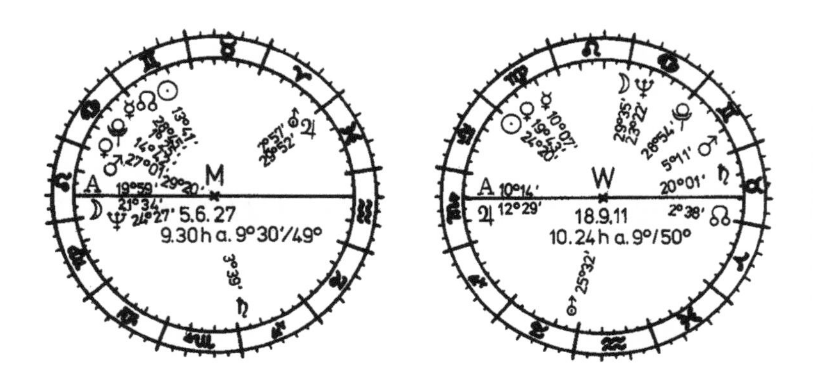

Fig. 18

Fig. 19

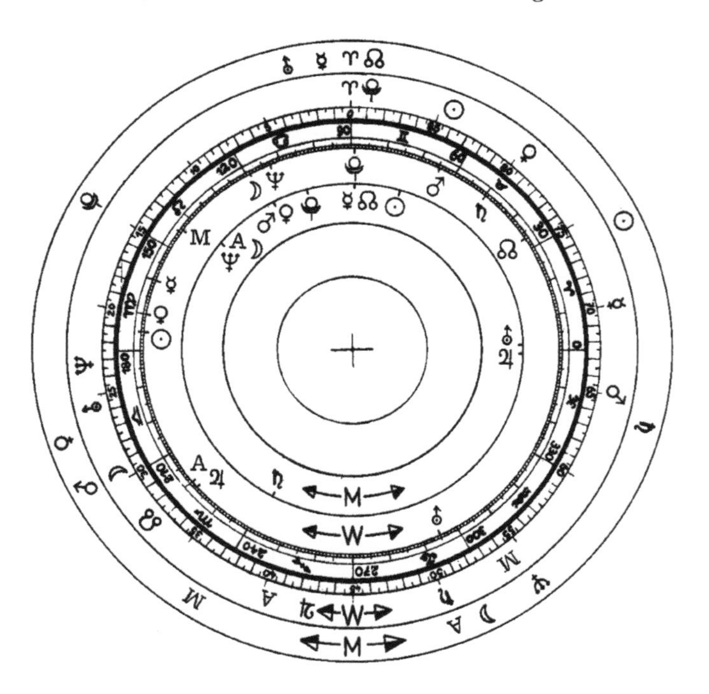

Fig. 20

Since in the case of transits a maximum orb of 1° is allowed, it follows that joint instances of stimulated combinations are only possible when the angular relationships do not exceed this 1° limit. Formerly orbs were treated generously, large ones were accepted. For this reason, the author has stressed for many years—in contradiction to other authors—that when comparing charts almost exact aspects are essential.

In the 360°-circle, right at the top, we find Pluto = Node, Moon = Venus, Mars, MC = Neptune, Moon. If we want to take into consideration the cosmic conditions of the individual factors the 360°-circle will give very little information. For the real data to work with we need the 90°-circle. (Practical forms are now available of the Contact Cosmogram, on which several 90°-circles are concentrically combined. These make it possible to enter the positions of several partners or colleagues in the individual circles. A wide selection may be found, with many examples, in the book *The Contact Cosmogram*, Fig. 23.)

For the interpretation one may refer to the CSI, adapting the interpretations correspondingly. (See also *Regeln zur Vergleichsanalyse* an original work by the author, which, in violation of copyright, has been copied several times, in part word for word, or the book *Die kosmische Ehe*.)

When making comparisons between cosmograms of partners special attention should be paid to the following factors:

Sun = man, body, spirit, father.
Moon = woman, soul, mother.
Sun/Moon = friendship, marriage, parents.
Venus = love, erotic attraction.
Sun/Venus = physical love.
Moon/Venus = the loving, devoted woman, spiritual love.
Mars = energy, sexual functions.
Venus/Mars = sex-drive, sexual union, procreative power.
Sun/Mars = procreative power of the man.
Moon/Mars = procreative woman, the wife.

Jupiter = law, legitimate union.
Sun/Jupiter = bridegroom, husband, healthy man.
Moon/Jupiter = bride, wife, healthy woman.
Venus/Jupiter = happiness in love, understanding.
Mars/Jupiter = the successful decision, the will to get married, engagement, wedding.
Saturn = inhibition, separation.
Sun/Saturn = inhibited man, separation.
Moon/Saturn = inhibited woman, separation.
Venus/Saturn = coming down to earth, sorrow in love, separation.
Sun/Moon = Saturn: difficulties in marriage, separation, divorce.
Sun/Moon = Jupiter: happiness in marriage.
Sun/Moon = Mars: joint aims in marriage.
Sun/Moon = Venus: love-marriage.
Uranus = excitement.
Sun/Uranus and Moon/Uranus = reciprocal excitement.
Venus/Uranus = sudden love.
Sun/Moon = Uranus: excitement in the marriage.
Jupiter/Uranus = change of fate.
Neptune = false ideas.
Sun/Neptune and Moon/Neptune = sensitivity, false ideas about each other, misunderstandings.
Venus/Neptune = romantic notions followed by disappointment, wrong ways in love.
Mars/Neptune = irritability through weakness, dangers of infections, impotence.
Sun/Pluto and Moon/Pluto: the fight for privileges, for leadership in the community.
Venus/Pluto = unusual powers of attraction, seduction, to be temporarily "mad" about each other.
Noon's Node = unions.
Venus/Node = love-unions.
Mars/Node = to work together.
Jupiter/Node = happy union.
Saturn/Node = separation.
Uranus/Node = sudden union, excitements in the union.

Neptune/Node = secret unions, dissolution of a union.
Pluto/Node = fateful union, in which two people have come together as if through some inner force.

(Reference can also be made to the 166 combinations in *Kosmische Ehe* (31). In this book about 50 examples are discussed.)

This summary gives keywords, which are intended to help when interpreting the cosmogram, but which should not be considered as firm and fast rules.

The first important connection seems to be that between Moon (W) at 29°35' Cancer and Mars (M) at 29°20' Cancer. Close to the Moon (M) we find Venus at 27°01'Cancer. Here not only the female (Moon) and the male (Mars) principles come together, but also the man's Venus urges to a sexual union.

During the course of years the author has made an odd discovery. In very many cases we find the midpoints Venus/Mars (sexual union) in the cosmogram of partners in the same place. If, in the outer circle, on the left hand side, we determine the midpoint of Venus/Mars we find it lies at about 28°. On the right hand side at about 73°, we find the woman's Venus/Mars, where the man's Sun is also posited.

In the preceding chapters we have already shown that individual factors should never be considered singly. The cosmic condition as a whole must be considered. We than get the following picture:

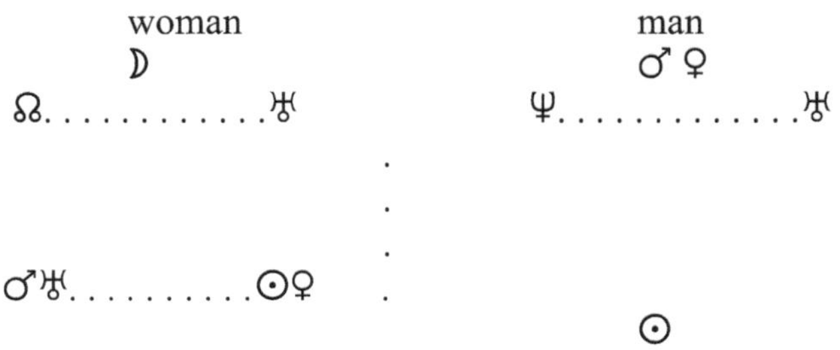

woman — man

☽ — ♂ ♀

☊............♅ — ♆.............♅

♂♅..........☉♀

☉

To be sure not to allow too large an orb we quickly compute a few half-sums:

Moon (W) = Uranus/Node = Sun/Mars-Venus/Mars
29°35' 29°05' 29°45' 27°27'

The deviation of Venus/Mars compared to the other factors only just exceeds 2°. Now what hidden interpretation lies in this planetary picture?

Moon = Uranus/Node: quickly becoming enthusiastic about other people.
Moon = Sun/Mars: the will to get married.
Moon = Venus/Mars: the urge to get married.

Through enthusiasm for or understanding of another person, the will to get married is engendered.

Mars (M) = Sun = Venus/Mars = Uranus/Neptune
29°20' 28°41' 28°10' 28°42'

(The degree numbers have been given conformity by the occasional use of their semi-squares.)

Mars = Sun: the procreative male.
Sun = Venus/Mars: sexual instinct.
Sun = Uranus/Neptune: easily influenced.
Mars = Uranus/Neptune: lack of self-control, misguided energy.

If in addition we consider the fact that the woman is 16 years older than the man, there is justification for the assumption that the man was easily influenced and became the tool of the woman.

In the 90° circle Saturn (W) and AS (M) are in the same place. In the 3 60°-circle this could not be determined so quickly, since these factors were in square. As you can see, the 90°-circle affords a much quicker grasp of the angular relationships. We now get the following planetary pictures:

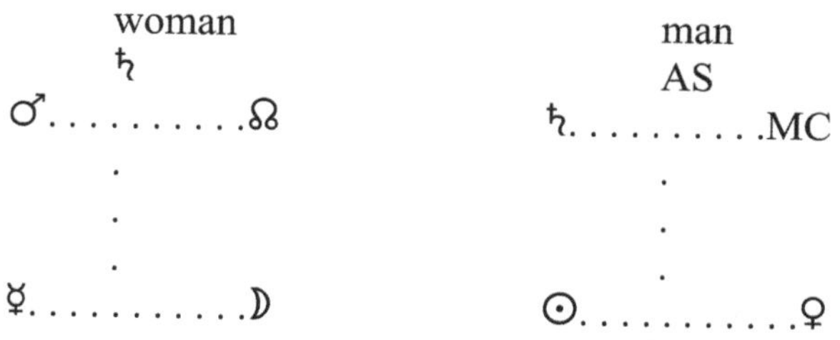

woman
♄
♂..........☊
.
.
.
☿...........☽

man
AS
♄..........MC
.
.
.
☉...........♀

The Saturn (W) = AS (M) contact in itself indicates a tendency to an estrangement or a separation, which becomes even stronger when we examine these aspects:

Saturn (W) = Mars/Node: separation of a sexual union.
Saturn = Moon/Mercury: to say good-bye, separation.
AS (M) = Saturn/MC: to suffer through others, separation.
AS (M) = Sun/Venus: reciprocal love.

While in the woman's chart the whole planetary picture points to a separation, we deduce from the male picture that in spite of mutual affection the one suffers through the other, and therefore the possibility of a separation exists.

Neptune (M) is conjunct MC (W). As the MC (W) is also Sun/Neptune (W) and Neptune (M) = Sun/MC, it is very likely that they did not see each other as they really were and a union had been built on false hopes. Mutual disappointment may lead to a separation.

Saturn (M) = Mars (W) further indicates that difficulties will arise in living together which may lead to the consideration of a separation. It would, however, be misleading, on the basis of such configurations, to speak of compulsory separation; for there are many marriages where bad planetary configurations in the cos-mogram do not lead to a separation. Religious, financial and other motives exercise their influence.

These examples may have shown how mutual aspects are inves-tigated. Here we should end the investigation of the radix charts, as it would lead us too far afield to interpret all contacts in detail. In-stead we shall examine the planetary configurations in operation at the time of marriage and at the time of separation.

The woman was born September 18, 1911. The love affair began in 1951. The woman was then 40, therefore the solar arc must have been about 40°. The solar arc for her birthday, September 18, 1951, is 39°30'.

The question of the relevant configurations at the time of meeting brings us to the problem of the ability to make contact at all. Most people do not find it too difficult to make contact with the opposite sex when they are young. Once a woman approaches 40 it is no longer so easy to find a suitable mate. Neither magazine advertisements nor marriage bureaux are of much use, if there is no cosmic foundation pointing to possibilities of contact leading to a marriage and a family.

When making such an investigation, one should not just consider the current angular relationships but consider the birthchart as a dynamic whole, as a fingerpost, not stationary but in constant motion. It is in this point that the cosmobiological investigation differs from the astrological one. We do not want to read a horoscope like cards or dreams. We aim to form our conclusions from the movements shown in the cosmogram, comparing them with the actual life and with it, the progression from the past into the future, using the examples of other similar situations as a further basis for comparison.

In the birth-chart of the woman born on September 18, 1911, we again pick out, in connection with the progressed factors, those configurations that catch the eye at once, because these form a clear correspondence between the birth constellations and the momentary picture of directions (Fig. 21).

On the left hand side, Venus s is conjunct Moon. This indicates the loving and devoted woman, who is longing for fulfillment of her womanhood. We recall the investigation of the Moon's position, according to which the desire for marriage can ensue from liking and understanding. As Venus s is on Mercury/Pluto s, love (Venus) problems (Mercury/Pluto) may arise. On the other side,

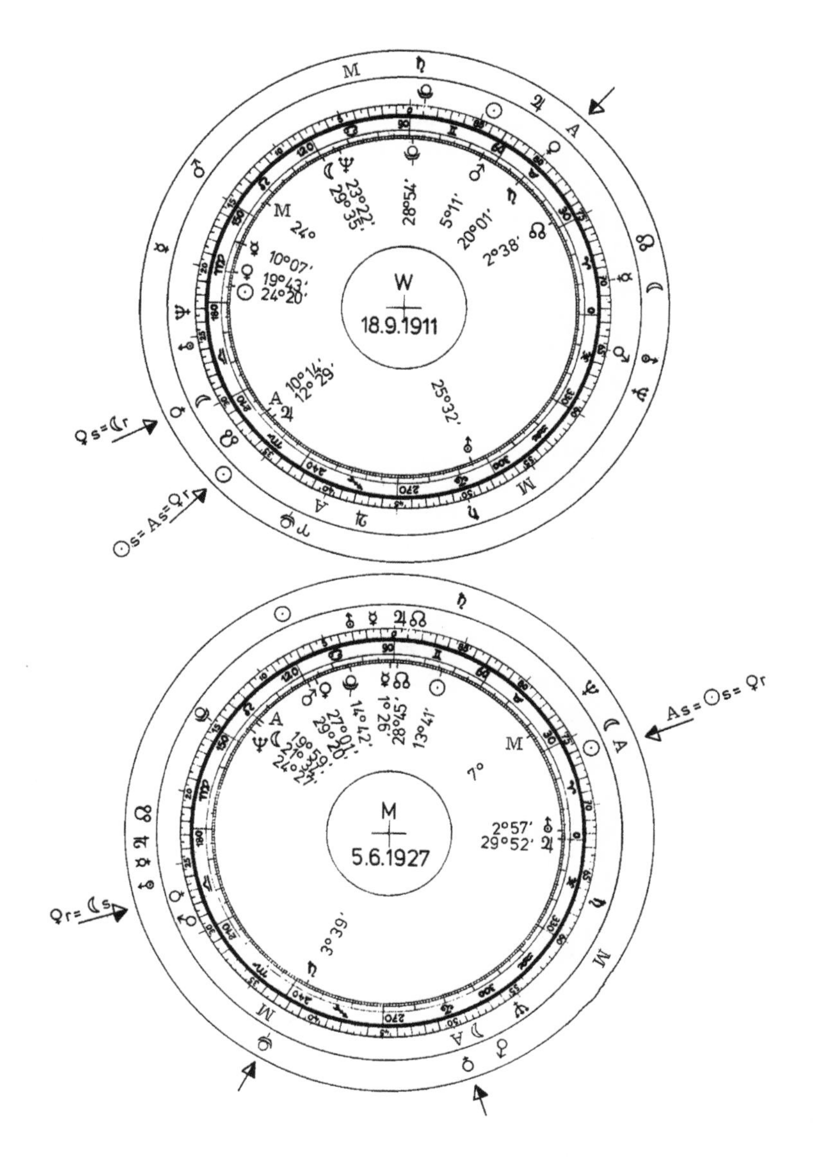

Fig. 21 (above) Female birth, directions

Fig. 22 (below) Male birth, directions

we see Venus is on Moon/AS with the renewed indication of a love relationship.

Considering the immediate vicinity of Venus s, we see that Venus passed Uranus r a few years ago. Here we also have a Moon/Neptune contact, therefore we may assume that through Venus s conjunct Uranus r an acquaintanceship is made, which carried a tendency to disappointment through the Moon/Neptune connection. Therefore, the wish to get married at all costs appears to be even much stronger. Let us direct Venus further ahead and we will see that in about three years (1° = 1 year) Venus s becomes conjunct Moon's Node. This coincides with Jupiter/Neptune = Uranus/AS, pointing to excitement, changes, false hopes. Traditionally it has always been assumed that the North Node has a linking and the South Node a separating tendency. This rule has proved to be incorrect. There was no reason why this should be so. The Nodes are not planets but points of intersection between the ecliptic and the lunar cycle. One cannot see why the character should change if North or South Nodes move in different directions. However, in each case it is decisive what connections the Nodes are forming with other factors. With Jupiter they will obviously yield a favourable influence, with Saturn a separating one, etc. Thus this constellation concerns a love (Venus) union (Node).

As the second important configuration we have AS s conjunct Venus (above right). Accordingly, Venus s not only stimulates the Moon, but Venus r is also stimulated by the progressed Asc. If we now place the indicator of the degree disc on the point, we will see Sun s exactly opposite, so that Venus r is also stimulated by Sun s. Investigating the cosmic conditions of these factors we have: AS s = Sun s = Saturn/Node s = Moon/MC s = Venus/Pluto s Venus r = Mercury/Pluto = Jupiter/Uranus = Moon/AS r.

If we look up these constellations in the CSI we get the following pointers:

AS s = Venus: love relationship.
Sun s = Venus: physical love.

These factors are now combined with the existing midpoints:

Saturn/Node s = AS s: inhibition, isolation, separation.
= Sun s: separation.
= Venus r: inhibitions in the love-life, insufficient adaptability.
Moon/MC = AS s: personal attitude to others.
= Sun s: spiritual and physical union of a woman.
= Venus r: strong affection.
Venus/Pluto s = AS: unusual love-affair.
= Sun s: strong affection, peculiar fate in love.
= Venus r: excessive or abnormal relationship.
Mercury/Pluto r = AS: influencing other people.
= Sun s: wishing to gain recognition.
= Venus r: peculiar love problems.
Jupiter/Uranus r = AS s: happiness as a couple.
= Sun s: sudden physical happiness.
= Venus r: to be quickly inflamed, engagement.
Moon/AS s = AS s: relationship of the woman to her environment.
= Sun s: personal contact, community (living together).
= Venus r: to adapt oneself because of love.

Summing up these interpretations, we do get many indications of contact, affection, love. The negative meanings are in the minority.

A lot of work may be involved in putting all these interpretations together. But by weighing up the quantity of positive and negative interpretations one does get a modicum of certainty. If one has investigated many cosmograms oneself, one will grasp the essential constellations immediately and be able to understand the whole situation without having to write down every single fact.

Close to the constellations we have just discussed, we find Jupiter s on the midpoint of Sun/Venus. "Wanting to possess a loving husband. Happiness in love" says the CSI. There is also Jupiter s = Moon's Node/MC (soul communion) = Sun/Pluto s. (Self-assertion) = Saturn/Neptune r (sensitivity, narrow-mindedness, egoism), to be taken into consideration.

On the right hand side, Uranus s is conjunct Mars r. If the indicator of the calculating dial is placed on this point, one will see Mercury exactly opposite. Simultaneously, several midpoints are involved. We have the following aspects:

Uranus s = Moon/Neptune s = Pluto/MC s = Mercury s.
Mars r = Venus/Saturn r = Jupiter/Pluto r.

From these we get the following interpretations:

Moon/Neptune s = Uranus s: following up sudden ideas or hunches.
= Mercury s: introspection guided by reason.
= Mars r: weakened natural powers in respect to sex-life. irritability.
Pluto/MC s = Uranus s: wishing to achieve one's aims with irresistible force.
= Mercury s: striving for recognition, powers of suggestion.
= Mars r: striving for power, the urge to dominate.
Venus/Saturn r = Uranus s: a very strong temporary infatuation.
= Mercury s: narrow-mindedness (or selfishness) in love.
= Mars r: weakened powers of procreation, separation.
Jupiter/Pluto r = Uranus s: sudden change.
= Mercury s: the desire to influence others.
= Mars r: to inspire others to enthusiasm.

These interpretations show indeed that the woman tries with all her strength to achieve her aims.

Further positions give us the following correlations:

Saturn s = Pluto has already been passed.
Saturn s = Mars/Uranus: separation.
MC s = Mars/Jupiter/s = Sun/Neptune s = Mercury/Uranus r = Mars/Moon's Node = Jupiter/MC: The I (MC) endeavors to understand the connections (Mercury/Uranus) to act correctly and successfully (Mars/Jupiter), without always

being positively attuned, (Sun/Neptune). It is directed towards a sex-partnership, marriage (Mars/Node), in order to be happy (Jupiter) oneself (MC).

(Aspects of the MC should always be considered of great importance, if one can be sure that the MC is correct. This position has to be confirmed by repeated investigations regarding past events).

MC r = Mars/Jupiter r = Sun/Neptune r = Mercury Uranus r (as above but r) = Mars/MC s = Mercury/Saturn s = Moon/Pluto s: consciousness of purpose (MC-complex) is combined with the power of perseverance (Mars/MC) and experience (Mercury/Saturn) with a fanaticism coloured with feeling (Moon/ Pluto).

Mars s = Venus/Saturn s= Venus/AS = Mercury/Saturn r = Mars/ MC: Against her own judgement, the native strives towards the fulfillment of her love desires.

Pluto s = Mars/Neptune s = Saturn/AS s =Neptune/MC r = Moon/Saturn r = Sun r = Venus/Pluto r: through an excessive sex-urge (Venus/Pluto) coupled with a desire to dominate a man (Pluto = Sun) she is trying to overcome many doubts and difficulties.

As has been emphasized before, it is absolutely essential to take also the prevailing circumstances into consideration. We do know that the woman is the senior partner by 16 years and that she is entering the age of menopause. With the slowing down of the functions of the germcell glands a change takes place within the woman often accompanied by deep depressions, nervous disturbances and irritability. Therefore, it is understandable if the woman is now going out to spend happy years with a partner, before the time of change is upon her. On the other hand, we have to consider that a young man who wishes to marry a considerably older woman is likely to regard her more as his mother than his wife. Supposing he no longer has a mother and was compelled to live among strangers in his young years at which time the protective care needed was not to be had, he most certainly will appreciate the value of a woman ready to give not only marital love but also maternal affection and protection. These points have always to be considered whenever there is a considerable difference in age. That does not mean, however, that these problems should always predominate. Indeed, there are many marriages with a great difference in age which can undoubtedly be described as happy.

Investigating the solar arc directions of the partner, we discover to some extent very similar configurations. Below right, we find Venus s = AS in exact opposition to the Sun; on the right, Moon/AS is conjunct Sun r and Venus r directly opposite; below left, Pluto transits the MC. The following configurations are in agreement:

woman (Fig. 21)	man (Fig. 22)
Venus s= Moon r	Venus r = Moon s
AS s = Venus r = Sun s	AS s = Venus r = Sun r

It is significant that individual configurations in both cosmograms are in the same place, although we do have to accept a slight deviation into the bargain.

The planetary pictures are not identical, but frequently they do depict the same meanings. We again begin with those aspects that catch the eye at once:

Venus s = AS r = Sun/Venus r = Sun/Mars r = Moon/Uranus s: A love relationship (Venus = AS) leads to physical love (Sun/Venus = Sun/Mars) with an energetic woman (Moon/Uranus).

AS s = (Moon s) = Sun r = Venus/Mars r = Neptune/Uranus r = Sun/Venus s = Pluto/Nodes. The aquaintanceship (AS) with a woman (Moon) leads to physical love (Sun/Venus) through being easily influenced (Uranus/Neptune) and the forceful influence (Pluto/Node) exercised by the woman.

On the left, Uranus s is approaching Venus and in the following years midpoint Venus/Mars = Sun and Mars. This indicates strong excitability where love is concerned. Danger exists to act prematurely through increased sensitivity without being fully conscious of the consequences. Pluto and Uranus in connection with Venus often lead to a whirl of excitement in love, an infatuation, only lasting a short while, giving place to an even ruder awakening.

Pluto s forms an aspect to MC r. Therefore we may assume that a big change in the affairs of this young man is going to take place. This change comes about through a love-experience, because Pluto s = Venus/Uranus s and MC r = Sun/Mercury. Accordingly, the young man (MC), who at other times is perfectly capable of independent thinking (Sun/Mercury) gets himself into a state of high excitability by being madly in love (Pluto = Venus/Uranus). This constellation is duplicated, since we also have MC s = Pluto r = Venus/Uranus r.

The best comment in these constellations is Goethe's citation: "Halb zog sie ihn, halb sank er hin" (roughly translated: they met halfway in that she pulled and he fell).

As the other constellations are very similar in their interpretation, we shall omit their explanation and look into a different method of investigation.

The Contact Cosmogram

This is a development of mine of recent years. The contact cosmogram simplifies working procedure in that it is completely separated from the 360°-circle and is limited to several concentric 90°-circles. The KK chart (from the German Kontakt Kosmogramm) makes it possible to compare as many as eight different cosmograms simultaneously. In addition to this, the main purpose of the contact cosmogram, one of the circles should be left vacant for entering current positions as well.

In Fig. 23, the outer circle presents the man's positions, the inner one the woman's positions. In addition, the transiting planets for January 1954 have been entered, that is for the time when the separation took place. One can see below right how Pluto transits the "disappointment" configuration MC (W) and Neptune (M) at about 54°. We have previously pointed out this mutual relationship; there was the fear that they did not see each other in a true light. This has now been shown uncompromisingly by the Pluto transit.

Between 36° and 40°, Saturn transits MC (M) and AS (W), indicating emotional depression in both partners. Mars transits the same points and joins Pluto t over Neptune (M) and MC (W) at the end of the month. Examining the sides opposite as well, we realise that MC (M) coincides with Sun/Venus (M). Saturn transiting these will break up a love relationship if it is not built on sufficiently secure foundations.

Neptune t, which often disappoints and undermines, passes over the common points Uranus (W) and Venus (M), and later also

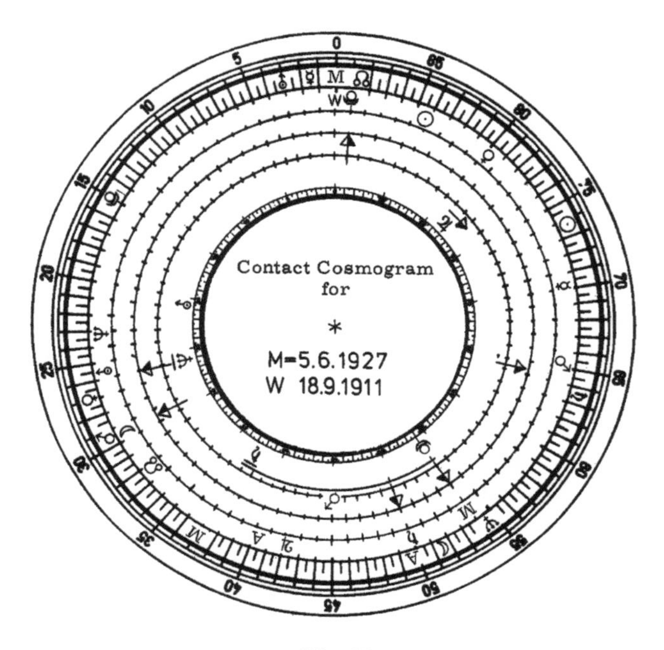

Fig. 23

over the Moon (W) and Mars (M) and in opposition to the Sun (M). Here we have the reason for the hope of there being a renewal of the love relationship in the near future. Let us also recall that Venus/Mars (W) is opposite. At this point the sexual relationship is dissolved by transiting Neptune. Of course, the configurations cannot be said to be the cause of this happening. There is, however, a correlation between the configurations and the events with a tendency to estrangement and separation. It is possible that after a prolonged separation they might come together again, when the negative trends have passed. Nevertheless one has to consider that the woman will not only have become older, but also that the difference in their ages will be much more pronounced, the young man being in the prime of life.

We are unable to compute the configurations for the first lovers' meeting, because we do not have the exact date. It is advisable first to compute the solar arc directions and then the transits. In this way, we get a confirmation by two different methods. One supports the other.

At the time of parting, several directions operate. We want to mention just a few and then leave it to the reader to examine them more closely.

woman	man
MC s = Saturn	MC s = Saturn
Neptune s = Mars	Mars s = Neptune
Uranus s = Neptune	Uranus s = Mars
	= Sun

It is no accident that we have similar configurations in both cos-mograms. On principle I do not use selected cases, but render those that have occurred in practice.

Computing The Day of an Expected Birth

For various reasons it is often desirable to know fairly precisely when the new baby will arrive. The husband wants to be near his wife at this time, all sorts of preparations have to be made, one wonders if complications are likely. In the following case, a doctor wanted to know when the birth of his daughter's baby was to be expected.

To be able to calculate in advance when a certain event is to be expected we have first got to know the cosmic correlations for that particular event. Conception and birth respond to the following aspects and midpoints:

Sun/Moon = Venus	Sun/Venus = Moon
Sun/Moon = Mars	Sun/Venus = Uranus
Sun/Moon = Jupiter	Sun/Mars = Venus
Moon/Venus = Mars	Sun/Jupiter = Moon
Moon/Venus = Uranus	Moon/Mars = Venus
Moon/Jupiter = Mars	Moon/Pluto = Venus
Venus/Mars = Sun	Venus/Mars = Uranus
Venus/Jupiter = Moon	Venus/Uranus = Sun
Venus/Pluto = Mars	Venus/Node = Mars
Venus/AS = Sun	Venus/MC = Mars
Mars/Jupiter	Mars/Jupiter = Sun
Mars/Jupiter = Venus	Mars/Jupiter = AS
Mars/Jupiter = Moon	Mars/Jupiter = Uranus

One should also pay attention to those configurations correlat-

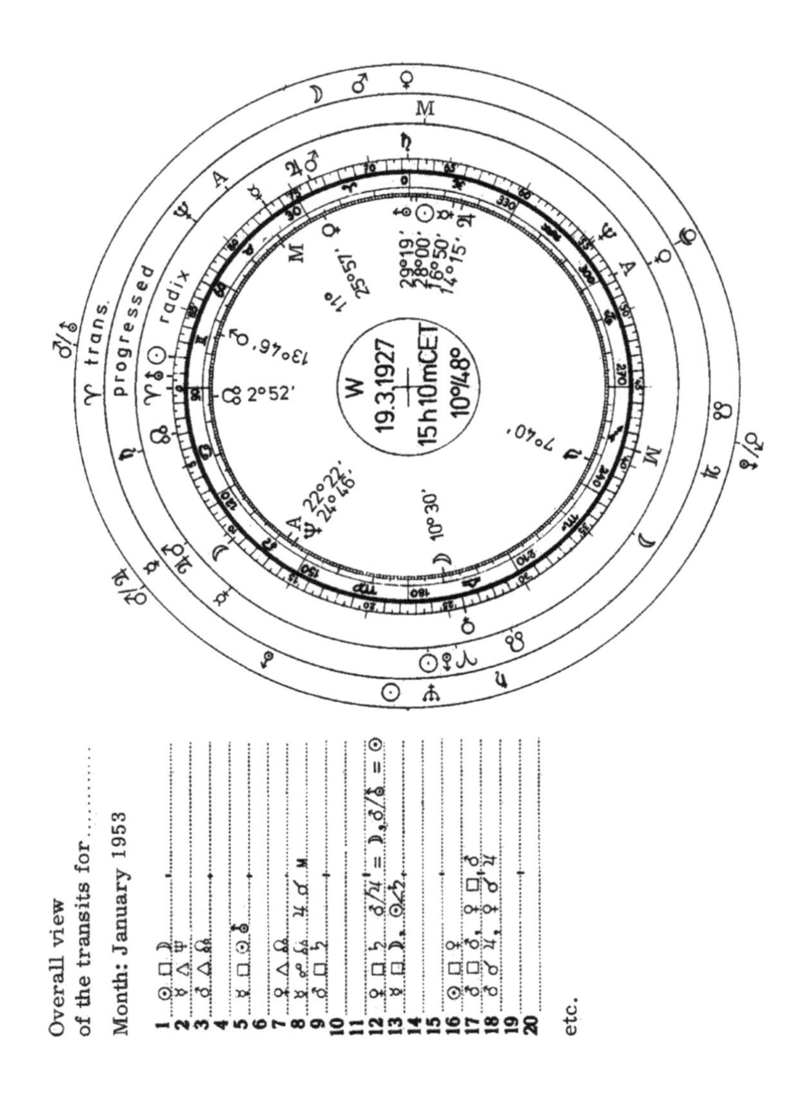

Fig. 24 Forecasting the birth of a child.

ing to operations. After all, a birth is a physical event somewhat like an operation. It may be found surprising that so many configurations have been mentioned, and yet. we have only included the most important ones. After all, we may get very different background situations, e. g. whether the baby is wanted and longed for or whether it just happened; is the mother completely well at this time, are there any difficulties in the home life, etc.

To begin with, we want a general idea of the year in question. Therefore, the solar arc is calculated and the larger disc moved forward by that number of degrees. Then the most important points correlating to a birth are investigated (Fig. 24).

In this case, the mother was born on March 19, 1927, at 15.10 CET at 10°E and 48°N. In January 1953, when the baby was expected, she was not quite 26 years old. The solar arc is 25°29'. In correlating the radical chart and the directed cosmogram we get the following aspects, the most important ones having been underlined:

Mars/Jupiter = Neptune r: delay or difficulties with birth (is not due until about 1/4 of a year after the expected birth.)
Jupiter s = Saturn/MC: to cling to hopes.
Uranus = Sun/Venus: love talk.
Mercury s = Mars/MC: to make arrangements.
Uranus s = Moon/MC: psychological crisis, birth (it is best to allow a slightly wider orb for aspects to the AS and MC, in case these points are not absolutely correct).
Uranus s = Mars/Saturn r: a test of nervous strength, intervention by force majeure (this is due a little later).
Venus r = Sun/Node s: love-union.
Node s = Mars/Jupiter r: a happy union (aspect has passed).
Moon s = Sun/Mars r: woman's will to live, vitality and vigour.
Moon s = Sun/Jupiter: happy experience of husband and wife.
MC r = Venus/Node s: intense love.
Venus s = AS r: loving attitude.
Venus s = Moon/Node r: thoughts of love.
Venus s = Mercury/Venus r: loving attitude, affection.

Jupiter r = Neptune/MC s: full of hopes, dreams of happiness.
Mercury r = Mercury/Venus s: thoughts of love.
AS s = Sun/Saturn r: difficulties, to feel misunderstood or not understood.
AS s = Moon/Neptune r: contact with sick people (stay in hospital or maternity home).
AS s = Venus/MC r: personal affection.
Sun r = Moon/Venus s: connubial love.

In this interpretation, several configurations indicate a birth, and others show the psychological condition of a young woman expecting a baby.

These notes give us an insight into the general situation as depicted by the solar arc directions. These, however, are usually released by the corresponding transits. For this reason, we have drawn an additional circle in our chart (Fig. 24) in order to show the transits for one month along with the directions. (Later on we will be discussing the usefulness of the magnetic 90°-dial in just this sort of case, as it enables the transiting planets to be moved effortlessly for each day under consideration).

For the transiting planets it is best to place an additional third disc underneath which is roughly 1.5-2 cm larger than the disc with the progressed factors.

One will now observe transiting Saturn opposition Venus r which, as a "hindrance" configuration, has already been passed in the beginning of January. The stimulating transit Uranus t trine Node has also been passed. According to the author's experience, trines and sextiles are of no great importance at births.

Jupiter conjunct MC is due on the 8th. This usually correlates to success or happiness, in this case maternal bliss. Here we recall the direction MC r = Venus/Node s. Therefore, this is likely to mean happiness in a love relationship, in marriage. Let us also examine the MC in the radical chart itself. We then get the planetary picture MC = Moon/Mars. Translating this equation we may say: I (MC) am becoming (Mars) a mother (Moon). Naturally, such configurations can only be confirmed if the MC is exact, that is, if the birth time is known correctly to within 4 minutes. An orb of several days will have to be allowed for transiting Jupiter. Mercury and Venus aspects are generally very weak. Less pleasant is the square of Mars to Saturn on the 9th. If possible, the birth should not be induced at this time; there is the possibility of some difficulties occurring for the mother. One should not always fear the worst under such transits. After all, hardly any child is born without some sort of physical pain, although all sorts of methods are employed today which considerably ease a confinement, and the more severe pains are avoided. Of particular importance appears to be Mars square Mars with Venus square Mars on the 17th and Mars conjunct Jupiter with Venus conjunct Jupiter on the 18th. Our initial deduction, therefore, is that the birth is likely to occur between the 8th and 18th.

For the more detailed work it is best to use the graphic 45° ephemeris or, better still, the 45° midpoint ephemeris, an extract of which is reproduced in Fig. 25. The linear 45° division corresponds to the 90°-circle. The advantage of this is, that all angles divisible by 45° coincide. On the left hand, we have the division into 45° degrees (partly interrupted by the inserted bodies of the birth chart). At the top is marked the month, January 1953 in this case. In the open field run the orbits (depicted as lines) of the individual transiting planets. The most important midpoint lines are shown by dotted lines. The positions of the stellar bodies at birth are entered in the degree division on the left, an exactly horizontal line is drawn from each planet to the right. These horizontal position-lines of the planets at birth intersect the orbit lines and the midpoint lines of the transiting planets at certain points. These points have been marked with circles and numbered.

At No. 1, the transiting Pluto intersects the ascendant-line. This, however, does not happen until the end of the month. One cannot expect the slow-moving planets to mark the occurrence of an event, for this we look to the fast-moving ones. Pluto transiting over Ascendant means changes in the environment. Those having experienced the changes and upheavals caused by the arrival of a new baby in the family will confirm the truth of this transit. The vertical line within the month marks the 12th of January. Mercury cuts the Ascendant line a few days earlier, and Sun/Mars crosses the Ascendant line a few days later.

At No. 2, we find a typical birth configuration. The midpoint Mars/Jupiter passes over the Moon; according to CSI, this means: "to become a mother, birth." Shortly before, the midpoint Mars/Moon's Node transits the lunar position, which is interpreted thus: a community of women (maternity home). At No. 3, Mars passed over Saturn a few days earlier; now on the 12th-13th Sun and Venus transit Saturn. Such a configuration is typical for a separation (Saturn) of one body (Sun) from another, that is, the child from the mother. Therefore one must by no means see something unfavourable in such a combination. At No. 4, the Venus position will be transited by Mars a few days later. These planetary configurations are frequently found in the cosmograms of mothers at birth. At the beginning of the month Saturn has already completed its transit over the Venus position. At No. 5, the transiting midpoint of Jupiter/Uranus (happy turn of events: the "thank the Lord" position) cuts through the Mars and Jupiter position-lines. One will note how time and again Mars and Jupiter play a big part in birth configurations, at (2) Mars/Jupiter = Moon, at (5) Mars = Jupiter = Jupiter/Uranus. At (6) the transiting midpoint Sun/Ju-piter (physical happiness) is aspected with Venus r and signifies a positive approach to life. At No. 7, Jupiter moves over the MC and so marks a personal success, the happy conclusion of a personal event. As has been mentioned before, operation configurations are often in evidence at the time of birth, without necessarily meaning an operative intervention as such. At (8) the operation significator Mars/Uranus meets the Sun. In CSI we find the following explanation for Sun = Mars/Uranus: sudden change in life, injury, accident, operation (birth). Observing Jupiter's orbit, we note that it is moving towards the Sun. This is of importance; it indicates that the mother will be well after the birth, complications are not to be feared.

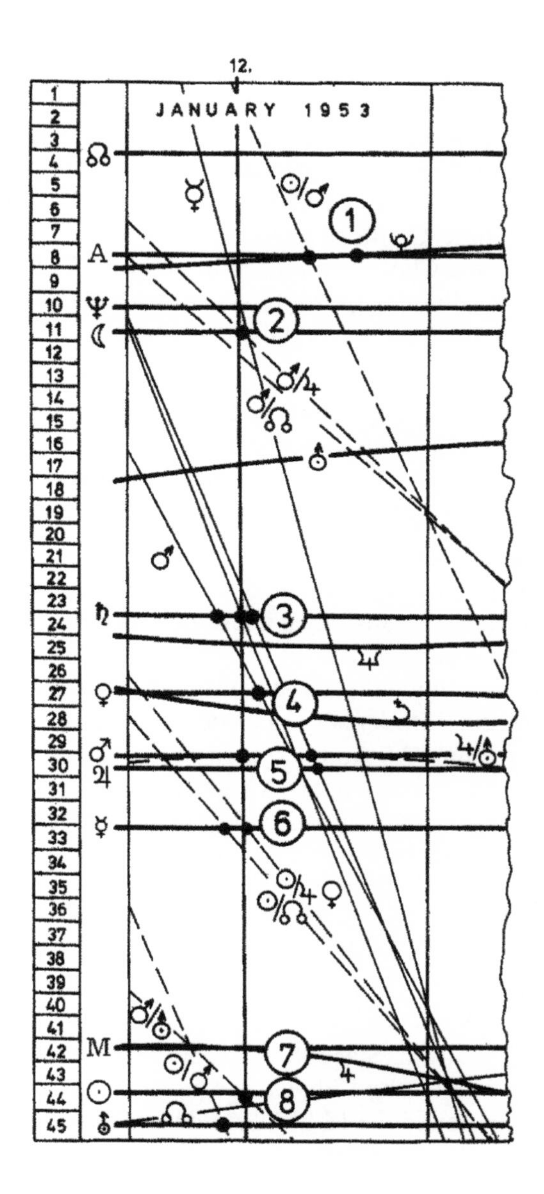
12.
JANUARY 1953
A
M
1
2
3
4
5
6
7
8
9
10
11
12
13
14
15
16
17
18
19
20
21
22
23
24
25
26
27
28
29
30
31
32
33
34
35
36
37
38
39
40
41
42
43
44
45

Fig. 25

After this explanation one might think that one could rely solely upon the graphic ephemeris. But this is not so. We are dealing here with two different methods, each complementing the other. In the graphic ephemeris one sees clearly how the various configurations develop and when they become due, one is able to observe a whole period of time. On the other hand, midpoints are difficult to recognise, as is the whole cosmic condition of the birth-chart. The MC has special significance for this confinement as it forms an almost exact axis with the Sun and therefore is also on Moon/Mars.

However, the graphic ephemeris does show the cosmic condition of the transiting planets up to a certain point. Around the 12th of January, transiting Mercury in the axis Mars/Jupiter has a completely different character compared to that on the 21st when aspected with Neptune or a few days later with Saturn.

If one wanted to come to the same conclusion as that reached with the graphic ephemeris, but using the dial only, one would have to mark the transiting planets for each single day and examine each day separately. Transiting Mars ranges between Saturn r and Mars r. Examining the movements of the transiting Mars, one will find the 12th-13th January Mars on Sun/Ascendant (power to succeed) = Uranus/AS (to be injured or wounded) = Moon/Node (a psychological experience) = Venus (love). The indication of an injury (birth) together with the power or strength to be successful (to expel the child) points to this day as the day of birth. Around the 15th, Mars is at 12° = Sun/Neptune (weakened physical body), around the 16th Mars = Uranus/Neptune (lack of vitality), around the 18th we find Mars, Jupiter = Mars/Jupiter (birth) = Neptune/Node (to be in the company of sick people). According to the transits of Mars, we have the possibilities of a birth around the 12th and the 18th. Since there are some weakness configurations in evidence after the 12th, we can presume this indicates the birth will occur around the 12th followed by the usual weakness resulting from confinement as can be seen in the subsequent configurations.

Between the 10th and 18th of January, the Sun moves from 20°

to 28° Capricorn, aspecting the following midpoints:

10.1. Sun 20° = Uranus/MC (physical and emotional unrest)
= Mercury/Neptune (sensitivity).
12. 1. Sun 22° = Node/MC (physical and emotional connection).
= Saturn (physical separation).
16. 1. Sun 26° = Venus (physical love)
= Moon/MC (positive outlook)
= Uranus/AS (physical unrest)
= Sun/Neptune (weakness)
= Mars/Saturn (poor vitality, illness).

It is not easy to ascertain the correct day for the birth from the Sun position alone. However, those who know that Sun = Saturn (separation of bodies) is often found at the time of birth would settle for January the 12th as the most likely day.

The constantly changing transiting midpoints are even more difficult to ascertain. One will certainly examine Mars t/Jupiter and Mars t/Uranus and again come to the same conclusion: January the 12th. We then have Mars t/Jupiter = Moon and Mars t/Uranus = Sun. In ascertaining these midpoints one cannot of course wholly rely on the visual impression, it is wisest to make a check by means of a quick computation. At noon on the 12th Mars/Jupiter is at 10°23' Aries, the Moon r is at 10°30' Libra. Therefore, the transiting midpoint Mars/Jupiter = Moon r must be due on the 12th-13th.

On the 12th, Mars t/Uranus is at 12°59' Taurus, the Sun is at 28°00' Aries. This makes a semi-square with a difference of only one minute.

Whoever really follows and practically applies the investigations described here will confirm that the graphic 45° midpoint ephemeris provides an excellent auxiliary method of finding the day of a certain event.

These investigations indicate that the most likely day for the birth would be the 12th January. This in fact has happened. Our prediction has been confirmed. Of course, every birth presents slightly different combinations, just as the cosmograms of individual mothers differ. In addition, the external circumstances vary in each case. Is the young mother healthy or already weakened? Does she live happily with her husband or does she await the confinement of her child in seclusion. Is she well off or not. But even so, certain basic configurations will turn up again and again. For this reason, it is pointless to make just one investigation. One must gain experience. Under no circumstances should one rely on speculation and arbitrary rules. Here. too, the golden rule applies, to rely on those factors that have proved themselves and not on any sort of hypothetical theories.

Calculating the Day for an Operation

When the question of a favourable day for an operation is raised, we must first realise that the success or failure of the operation does not "depend on the stars." Our task is to use our calculations to help the patient and the surgeon. It is recognised in medical circles that operations do not generally follow the same course from one day to another. In south Germany the influence of the Fohn (a warm wind blowing off the alps from the south) is well known whilst in the USA a very extensive statistical survey has proved the influence of the Moon beyond question. It has been established in particular that more severe haemorrhages may be expected at full moon than at other times. We can show that other cosmic factors also have their effect.

However, on no account should the patient exercise pressure and say: "only on this day have I favourable configurations, you must operate on me then." There are cases where immediate intervention is essential and where the operation cannot be postponed. On the other hand, the surgeon should try to consider the patient's wishes as far as is practicable since a patient's positive frame of mind contributes to a successful outcome. The wife of a patient asked the surgeon not to operate on a certain day. The surgeon ignored her request and performed the operation at that time to prove to her the silliness of such a "superstitious" request. The patient died. Should the surgeon not constantly reproach himself for having operated on that particular day, just to prove that a house wife's so-called superstitious request was nonsense?

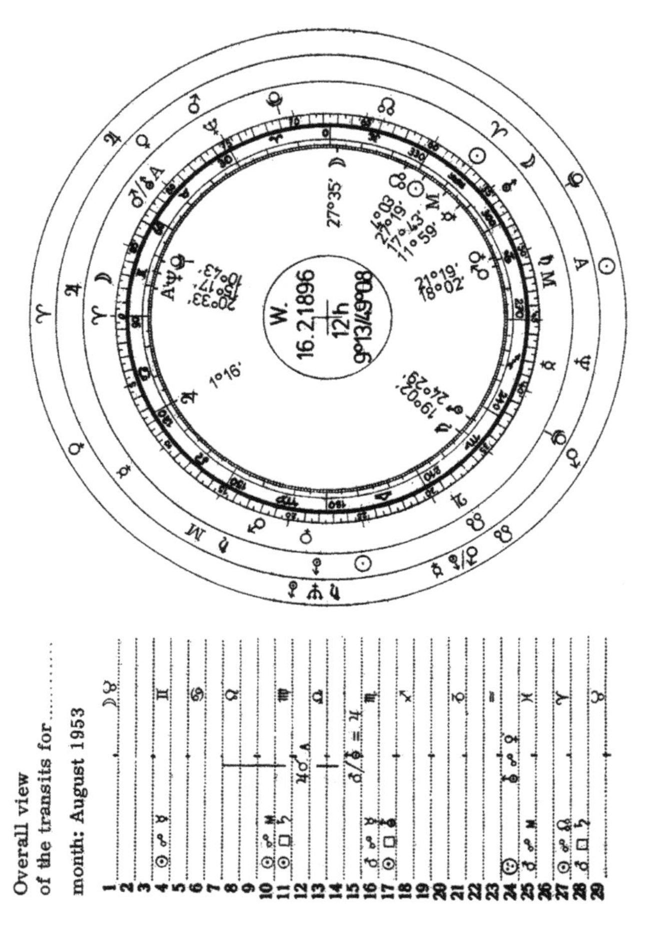

Fig. 26 Calculating the day for a surgical operation.

Many examples can be given where operations have been successful through a consideration of the cosmic factors.

However we should also point out that it is wrong to look only for "favorable" configurations. Every operation is an intervention, it is an injury inflicted on the body, which will bring some pain and discomfort. It is preferable to refer to "favorable correlations."

The following example case history is taken from a practice and was used previously as work problem No. 8 in *Kosmobiologie*:

Female; February 16, 1896, 12 Noon, 9°13’ E, 49°08’ N (Fig. 26). The native had to undergo a hernia operation in August 1953.

When dealing with enquiries relating to operations, the first factor to examine is the Mars/Uranus midpoint; this does not of course exclude other configurations that may be involved. In my experience, in the majority of cases the operation-axis (Mars/Uranus) is present.

In the above case, it lies at 21°15’ Gemini/Sagittarius or at 36°15’ and 81°15’ in terms of the 90°-circle. It falls almost exactly on the AS and not far from the Mars/Saturn axis, a combination which under certain circumstances may be fatal. The solar-arc for the time in question is c. 57°10’. Directed by this arc, Mars/Uranus s = Aquarius 18°25’, i.e. 48°25’ in the 90°-circle. This progressed midpoint has just passed over the MC, but has not yet reached the square to Saturn. These critical aspects demand special care and exactitude when making one’s calculations. Among the progressed factors the following are particularly prominent:

Sun s = Mars/Jupiter r: 24°29’ 24°30’	action promising success. It is important that Sun s does not receive critical aspects.

However:

Sun r = Mars/Pluto s: 27°19’ 26°32’	injury, accident, could also be surgical intervention. This aspect was exact in February 1953.

Simultaneously:

Sun r = Sun/Jupiter s: 27°19’ 11°28’ (26°19’)	Health, recovery, the contact between Sun and Jupiter may nearly always be considered as favourable to recovery.
Mars s = Neptune r: 15°12’ 15°27’	weakness, lack of energy (exact September 1953).
Jupiter s = Mars/Pluto r: 28°26’ 29°22’	luck when injured, i.e., successful operation.

Jupiter s = Sun/Jupiter r: prospect of good recovery.
28°26' 29°17' (= Mars/Pluto: through operation). This aspect is not due until June 1954.

Mercury s = Uranus r: renewal, change.
9°09' 24°29' (9°29')

AS s = MC r = Mercury/Uranus r: after deliberation (Mercury/
18°03' 17°43' 18°14' Uranus) drawing one's own (MC) conclusions and acting to repair a defect (AS = Mercury/Uranus).

Saturn r = Mars/Uranus s: serious injury, serious operation. This
19°02' 18°35' aspect is not due for another six months.

This summary gives most of the important configurations which point to an operation. The majority indicate a successful outcome. Of course, we also have to take the transiting planets into consideration. Next to the chart in Fig. 26, we see the overall picture of the transits for August 1953.

This overall survey is further simplified by using the 45° midpoint graphic ephemeris for August 1953. (Fig. 27). This shows the general cosmic situation. At the end of July Saturn and Neptune contact each other and in September Uranus and Neptune. In observing this, little attention is paid to the type of aspect formed. (Saturn conjunct Neptune and Uranus square Neptune); it is sufficient to know that their orbits stand in a certain relationship to each other. The operation, if it has to be undertaken in August should take place between those two meeting points. Unfortunately, these coincide with the Venus position in the birth chart, the Saturn/Neptune midpoint separates from Venus at the end of July, which means that the aspect is no longer exact.

Now let us evaluate the individual configurations, which have been numbered in Fig. 27. At No. 1, the MC is transited by the Sun. The following days are less favourable, as Sun moves over Saturn (2). At No. 3 Mars/Jupiter transits the Sun, which is also the position of Sun/Jupiter s = Sun r. This constellation is due shortly before the 10th of August. The same is valid for transiting Sun/ Jupiter = Mars (4) which maybe interpreted as will (Mars) to recover

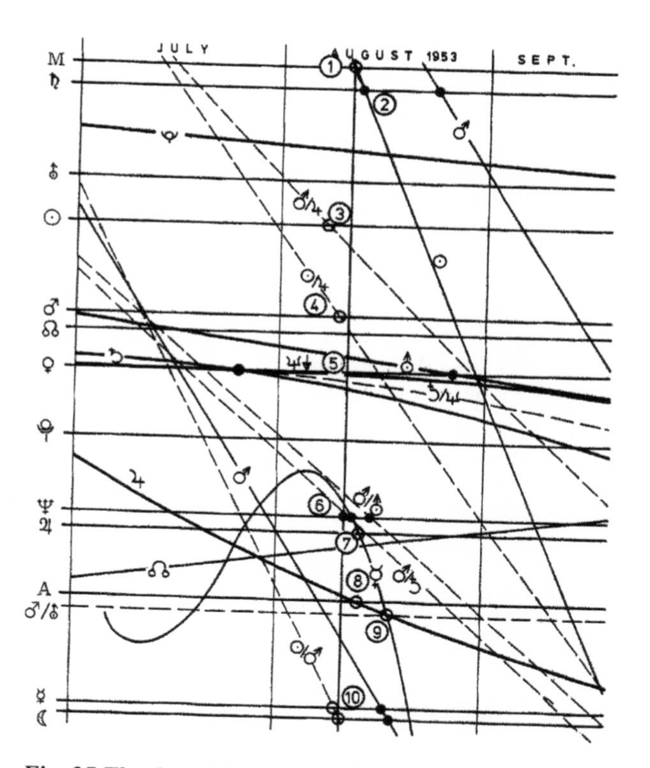

Fig. 27 The day of the operation in the graphic ephemeris

(Sun/Jupiter). Transiting Saturn/Neptune = Venus r has already been discussed (5). Mars/Uranus, the transiting operation axis aspects Neptune during the day after the 10th and then Mars. Mars t/Saturn = Neptune (6) indicates a weakness. However, we have also Mars t/Saturn = Jupiter: "improvement in a sickness" providing "concentrated energy is applied" (CSI 703). Transiting Jupiter passes over the AS (8) and soon afterwards the axis Mars/ Uranus (9). This is the configuration which gives hope for a satisfactory outcome of the operation. Sun t/Mars = Mercury = Moon may be seen as readiness for action. Attention should now be paid to the fact that each configuration has a running-in period during which its influence is at its greatest; once it has become exact, one can no longer expect the same powerful influence. In Fig. 27 the constellations to be considered favourable are marked with a circle, the unfavourable ones by black dots. In this way we arrive at the best time for an operation as being about the 10th of August.

The following rules, which have to date always proved their worth should also be taken into consideration:

1. The transiting Moon should not be in the sign correlating to that part of the body which is to be operated on. For a hernia operation the corresponding signs are Virgo, Libra, Scorpio. This rule rests on the theory that the signs have a special affinity to certain parts of the body and organs: (32)

Aries: head (face, eyes, brain)
Taurus: neck (throat, tonsils, thyroid)
Gemini: shoulders, arms, hands, lungs
Cancer: breast (lungs?, stomach)
Leo: spinal cord and the region of the heart
Virgo: digestive tract (intestines, spleen, peritoneum)
Libra: kidneys and skin
Scorpio: excretory organs, reproductive organs
Sagittarius: hips, thighs
Capricorn: skeleton, knees
Aquarius: blood-circulation, calves (veins)
Pisces: feet

This table is only a rough guide. Anyone wanting to work in astro-medicine would be well advised first to study the relevant literature extensively, before endeavoring to act in an advisory capacity on any illness.

2. An operation should not be performed either just before new moon or just before full moon. At new moon we often get a lack of vitality and at full moon hemorrhages may present a danger, as has been confirmed by medical statistics.

3. One should avoid unfavorable aspects of Saturn, especially to Sun, as complications may set in. Angular relationships to Neptune are also best avoided, as these can at times indicate infections.

4. It is of special advantage to have favorable aspects between Sun and Jupiter after the operation, as these tend to be beneficial to a quick recovery.

It is of course never possible to avoid completely all unfavorable constellations, however, one should always choose a time when the health promoting aspects are in the majority.

According, to the above rules, the days just before the 9th (new moon) and those just before the 24th (full moon) cannot be considered. The Moon transits unfavorable signs for this operation (rule 2) between the 11th and the 16th. The 11th is best avoided because of Sun square Saturn. On the other hand, this constellation could correlate to the "inhibited body" after the operation, which is confined to bed, and is not yet allowed to eat everything, etc. The 10th remains as the best possible day. The aspects on the 16-17 are not favorable; we have then Mars opposition Venus and Sun square Moon in Scorpio. Uranus opposition Venus and Mars square Saturn are best avoided in the second half of the month.

We may now also enter the transiting planets on a third chart and investigate their contacts to the radix on the 90°-dial. We should point out that in the graphic ephemerides the midpoints of the birth configurations are not easily seen; one can easily be misled, because under certain conditions one may be dealing with angles of 22.5°, and not 45° based midpoints as might appear at first sight when examining the positions on the 45° graph. In Fig. 27 for example, one might assume that Venus r and therefore also Saturn t and Uranus t pass in the middle of Mars and Pluto. This is not the case, the midpoint Mars/Pluto lies at 29°22' Pisces, Venus is at 21°19' Capricorn, making no aspect.

The operation, calculated for August 10, 1953, was performed on that day. The native herself wrote afterwards: "The operation took place on the 10th August, 1953, between 8 a.m. and 11 a.m. During my three weeks' stay in hospital, I made very favorable progress. There were no complications of any sort. The time you recommended was therefore correct."

Based on this confirmation it is now also possible to investigate the position of the transiting Moon. The Moon at noon on 10.8.1953 was 26°441 Leo (41°44' on the 90°-dial) and was accordingly with the Moon s and Uranus r.

If you require further cases of operations for investigation, the numerous examples in the journal *Kosmobiologie* are recommended. Further, a hydrocele operation on an infant under Saturn conjunct Venus, a lung operation under Saturn opposition Neptune, a successful operation under Jupiter t = Jupiter r = Mars/Uranus and an operation which resulted in death under Pluto t = Saturn = MC r are given in the book *Die Jahreskurve*.

A Case of Illness

"With respect to a diagnosis, astro-medical significators merely correlate to certain morphological and functional factors in any illness. They do not describe an illness in the sense of modern medicine, as all and everything is judged from an endogenous point of view. " These words from Dr. Frhr. von Klöckler (33) have been used as a preliminary to counter any false conceptions to the effect that it may be possible to diagnose a disease from the cosmogram alone; the cosmogram is primarily an aid to diagnosis. Traditional astro-medicine has remained enmeshed in handed-down concepts, all its branches have not yet been scientifically investigated, as would be necessary. For this reason, it is essential to accept certain limitations in astro-medical diagnosis. Therefore, our task is to discover certain definite tendencies, simultaneously calculating when these may break out, so that preventive measures may be taken.

The case of sickness discussed here has been made available by Dr. Böck and has been investigated with his cooperation. It concerns a woman born on March 24, 1911, at 23.15 at 18°30'E and 50°19'N (Fig. 28).

This birth-chart indicates an introverted disposition, most of the significators being below the horizon. Above the horizon are only Jupiter, Neptune and Pluto. There being no indications to the contrary, such people tend to take things rather seriously; they live more within themselves and have fewer defenses against the outside world.

Some of the especially prominent aspects in this cosmogram

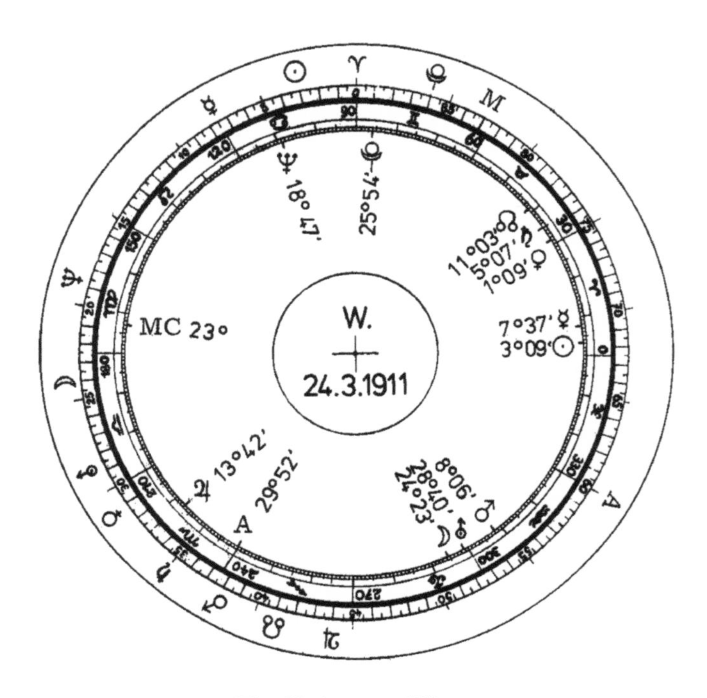

Fig. 28 A case of illness.

are: Mars square Saturn, Venus conjunct Saturn, Mars square Jupiter, Moon opposition Neptune, Moon conjunct Uranus. Traditionally, those parts of the body are particularly endangered which are tenanted by unfavorably aspected planets; the opposite signs will also have to be taken into account.

Taurus - Scorpio: Venus, Saturn, Jupiter, AS
Cancer - Capricorn: Neptune, Moon, Uranus

Taurus and Scorpio correspond traditionally to the neck region, reproductive and excretory organs.

Cancer and Capricorn correlate to the stomach, breast, knees and skin.

With these aspects an orb of up to five degrees has been chosen and which has only been exceeded slightly by the Moon. With the faster moving planets one may occasionally allow a larger orb but not with the slower ones, as these aspects maybe in operation for years. The opposition of Jupiter to Saturn has therefore not been taken into account.

The Sun, which is supposed to be the significator of health, has no other aspects than a conjunction to Mercury.

When the birth picture has been transcribed onto the 90°-circle, one should keep the individual aspects in mind, using the calculating-dial for a more detailed investigation in order to determine with which midpoints the individual factors correspond. Here the orbs should not be exceeded by much more than one degree. One has always to start from the principle that the effect of directions and transits is limited to about one degree on either side.

We arrive at the following interpretation:

Moon (Capricorn) - 180 - Neptune (Cancer: breast, stomach, lungs may be debilitated and susceptible, if other configurations join in. Under no circumstances should one try to make a diagnosis upon these foundations alone.

Neptune - 45 - Mercury/Uranus: nervous disorders.

Neptune - 90 - Sun/Saturn: inhibited mental development, psychological peculiarities, mental, emotional and physical crisis, hereditary taint.

According to the direct aspects, the Sun seemed "free of debilitating influences" but in the midpoint connections it is the Sun in particular that is in contact with those disease prone planets, Saturn and Neptune.

Moon - 90 - Uranus/Neptune: high sensitivity, period of debility.

Moon - 135 - Venus/Neptune: chaotic emotional life, impressionability, resigned, unhappy or disillusioned woman.

Here the psychological factor is involved too, as it is indeed the underlying cause for many an illness. Particularly in matters of love, a woman's disappointment often preys upon her health.

From the various indications we may deduce that the native is inhibited in her development, with the further complication of a hereditary taint, and that she is extremely sensitive and may occasionally have periods of debility. A disease, correlating to Moon - 180 - Saturn, was contracted at the age of 5, when the progressed Neptune was almost opposition Moon: Pneumonia was caught; the native ran a high temperature for 14 days. This was complicated by pleurisy. The midpoints of Moon-Neptune at birth were also stimulated by this direction.

Neptune s = Mercury/Uranus s = Sun/Saturn s=
Moon r = Uranus/Neptune r = Venus/Neptune r

This example shows clearly how the correlating tendencies of a constellation are realized in that year in which the factors concerned come into contact by direction.

A further confirmation of Moon - 180 - Neptune occurred on February 28, 1933, with a gastric hemorrhage. At this time, transiting Uranus was at 20°57' Aries almost exactly on the midpoint Moon/Neptune at 21°35' Aries. This simultaneously confirms the effectiveness of the midpoints. Because the occurrence did not take place at Uranus - 90° - Neptune nor at Uranus - 90° - Moon, but at Uranus = Moon/Neptune.

Let us now continue to examine the significators correlating to disease in this birth-chart:

Mars (Aquarius) - 90° - Saturn (Taurus): calves, varicose veins, heart conditions, neck region, genital organs.
Mars - 135 - MC - 90 - Saturn/Node: the desire to gain release from emotional depression, to stand alone, separation.
Mars - 135 - MC - 135 - Neptune/AS: lack of vitality, instinctive aberrations, unpleasant living together.

These constellations in their midpoint connections point rather to emotional suffering and lack of vitality than to physical illness. Here we must also remark that the native married on March 26, 1938. The marriage broke up in June 1939; divorce followed in 1943. The marriage took place under Sun s = Venus/Uranus (temporary affection), it broke up, when in July 1939 Neptune t was at 20° Libra and formed a semi-square to Saturn. (Without the dial. it is very difficult to recognize such configurations).

The marriage was dissolved under Sun s - 0 - Saturn r. Here we can see that certainly not all critical aspects have to refer to sickness, but they may indirectly do so, through emotional suffering; engendering a physical complaint. A heart condition which did not appear until 1953, when MC s at 5° Scorpio reached opposition Saturn, may be allied to this disappointment in the love-life.

There is a danger when using the 90°-dial of concentrating too much on the individual midpoints and thereby overlooking a basic aspect in the 360°-circle. Therefore, one should always keep in mind the positions of the planets within the zodiac circle.

Our initial investigation excluded the opposition of Jupiter to Saturn, because an orb of 8° is too wide for slow-moving planets. But if we place the indicator of the calculating disc in the middle of Jupiter/Saturn we find Mars at this point with a difference of just over 1°. Mars is the connecting link, so to speak, between Jupiter and Saturn. The angular relationships of Jupiter and Saturn correlate to diseases of the lungs, liver, gall-bladder and chronic conditions and to organic sluggishness. (Look up the biological correspondences under Jupiter/Saturn in the CSI.) The native suffered again and again from pneumonia, pleurisy and bronchitis developing into bronchiectasis. When these complaints appeared in February 1933, Saturn t was at 8° Aquarius in conjunction with Mars, that is, on the midpoint Jupiter/Uranus. With a similar condition in 1944, Neptune t corresponded with the opposition to the Sun (= Saturn/AS) and Saturn transiting square Sun r. The planets Saturn and Neptune, which in the radix point to sickness indicated illness by transits to the Sun, (signifying body). Additionally, Sun s = Mars/Saturn became due at this time.

Bronchiectasis appeared for the first time in 1939, when Pluto s - 90 - Saturn r was in operation. According to CSI, Saturn-Pluto connections correlate to organ underdevelopment, calcification or hardening of organs. Bronchiectasis is to be considered as an enlargement and malformation of the bronchi. One could make the objection that Pluto - 90 - Saturn will appear in the charts of many people in the same year. In this case, this configuration has personal significance, because in the birth-chart Pluto is square (with an orb of only 3°) to MC.

Furthermore we have the following angular relationships in this cosmogram.

Venus - 0 - Saturn (Taurus): malfunctions of the internal glandular secretions, bladder-stones, stones in the kidney or the gall bladder. Urinal obstruction, neck-complaints, diseases of the secretory organs.
Venus - 45 - Saturn/Uranus: tensions in love-life, separation.
Saturn - 45 - Venus/Mars: inhibitions in the love-life, pathological instincts, separation.

When in 1950, pyelitis, nephritis and kidney hemorrhages were contracted Saturn transited the middle degrees of the signs Virgo repeatedly, forming aspects of 135° to Venus and an aspect to Venus/Mars - 45 - Saturn and thus bringing the tendencies shown in the birth chart to the surface.

Our example has been taken from the practice and has in no way been "doctored". It is not as simple as some text-books will have it to make a diagnosis from the cosmogram. One should not forget that a causal connection is out of the question. If correlations to certain diseases are found in a cosmogram, it does not mean that they will necessarily materialize. The conditions must always be prevalent which will make it possible for such tendencies to manifest themselves. A great part is also played by the way of living and nutrition, which may favor one disease and help to avoid another. One can in no way rely on the signs and their correlations. There are certain degrees in the zodiac which again and again are in evidence with certain diseases. For instance, the first degrees of Libra and kidney complaints appear to be related. But there are also very many instances where the traditional correlations completely fail. In the preceding example one might have expected Libra to be heavily tenanted because of the kidney complaints. However, we do find the Sun opposing the first degrees of Libra. Further, Venus as the "kidney-planet" is afflicted by the conjunction to Saturn and is also on the midpoint Saturn/Uranus and, finally, Saturn is semi-square to Venus/ Mars.

On page 125 in the CSI we find under "biological correspondence" the interpretation "autonomous disorder" (particularly of the intestines and kidneys). Under the interpretations of the midpoints on the right-hand side in the CSI only occasional reference to diseases are made. One may, however, assume that in very many cases the biological correlations may apply, when the midpoint is tenanted by a negative factor and the rest of the cosmogram shows similar tendencies.

Experience is always the best foundation. Only he, who has compared many cosmic pictures of diseases, will eventually become sure and confident in the assessment.

The Versatile Magnetic Workboard

The 90° workboard for cosmobiological research already has a history behind it and has already undergone numerous changes. The first workboard was a cork slab with a work surface pasted over. With the help of planet needles the positions of the stellar bodies could be marked. Later came workboards of metal and of plastic. Experience was gained with these devices, and many difficulties overcome. The greatest difficulty was presented by the center hole for the bolt not being punched out precisely enough.

Finally, we developed the magnetic 90° workboard. Each single device had to be made by hand. Now we hope to have found a device that will meet most all requirements. This is a "magnetized drawing surface" which had been built to suit our purposes and which at the same time is suitable for work with the revolving 90° disc and also for working out the graphic 45°ephemeris.

The foundation of the device is the magnetic plate, which has a clamp along the left side. The plate is covered with the work surface, which is marked with a large 90° circle. A hole has been drilled in the center, where the bolt is to be inserted. The following operations are then possible.

1. Figuring the Radix. The calculation disc is laid exactly concentric ally onto an Ebertin K2 Form and the center hole is punched with the bolt. It is very important that the disc has been set onto the form exactly, that is all graduations precisely aligned. A steel punch can also be used (diameter 6 mm); in which case, a

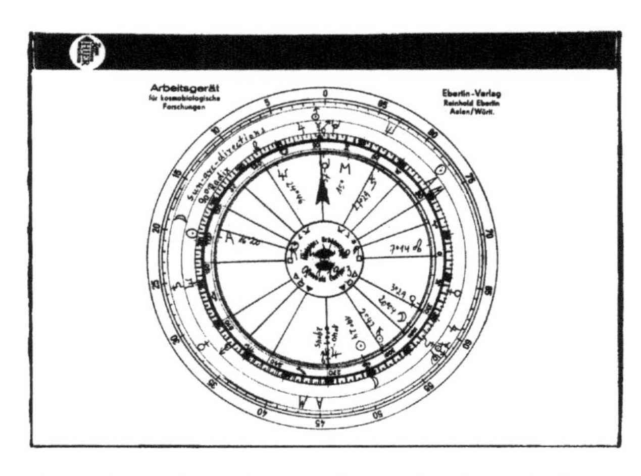

Fig. 1 shows the workboard, along the top the clamp, in the center the nut and bolt with 360°/90° Form and the planet magnets set around.

piece of strong cardboard is laid underneath, the form on top, the calculation disc set down exactly, the punch set at exact center, and with a tap of the hammer the correct hole is punched, through which the form can easily be fastened in place. The various entries can now be made in the form, first the symbols and then the positions, starting from the outside and working towards the center. The positions are also entered in the outer circle. On laying down calculation disc, which is fastened with the nut and bolt, the separate aspects in the inner circle can be determined by directing the arrow to the desired points and checking to see if there are any angular relations, e.g. an angle of 45° (semisquare), of 90° (square), of 135° (sesquiquadrate), 180° (opposition), etc. At the same time, the angular relations are entered in the form for "cosmic structural pictures" (KS 2 Form). What was said previously about aspects, orbs, etc. must be observed.

Now the arrow is directed towards the various positions in the 90° circle and the halfsums of each planet determined. At the same time, entries are made in Form KS 2. Using *Combination of Stellar Influences* the individual aspects are interpreted and notes made.

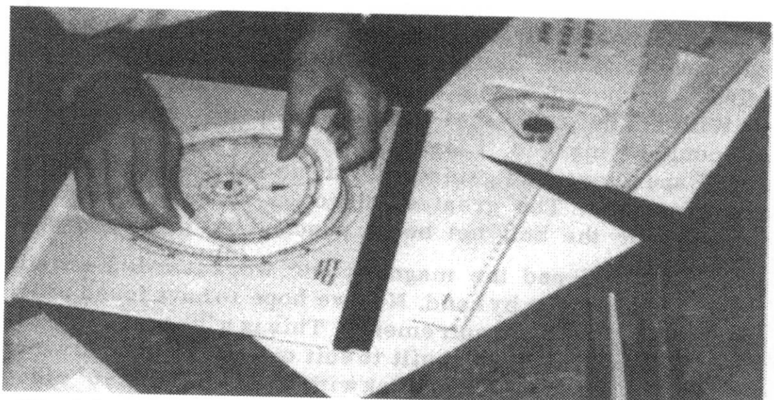

Fig. 2 demonstrates how to lay on the disc after the precise center hole has been punched through the paper. If a magnetic peg is used, it has to be pushed up from underneath.

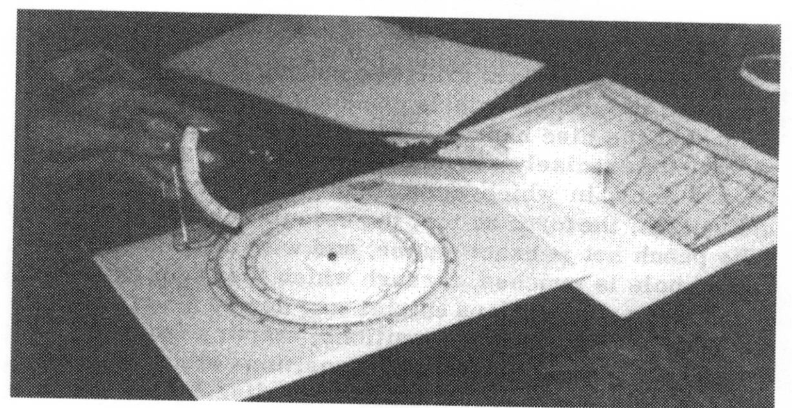

Fig. 3 shows the drawing device with the movable ruler, which can be screwed tight.

2. Using the Magnets. For a view of the positions of transiting planets the corresponding day is looked up in the ephemeris and the magnets placed accordingly on the points in the 90° circle. The diurnal constellations can thus be easily comprehended; care must be taken that the magnets are placed absolutely correctly in the 90° circle. To ensure correctness stickers can be glued on the work surface marking the zones 0-30° for Aries, Cancer, Libra, Capricorn,

30-60° for Taurus, Leo, Scorpio, Aquarius, and 60-90° for Gemini, Virgo, Sagittarius and Pisces.

The magnets can also be used for contact studies. They are placed in the correct positions according to the cosmogram of the partner and quick analysis can be made as to compatibility.

The heliocentric positions can also be marked by means of the magnets, but in this case it is advisable to lay a blank piece of paper under the radix to fill in the heliocentric positions.

The magnetized planets can be used for all ages for rough calculations and figuring out when certain directions are due.

For study of weather conditions or world events, the K2 Form is used, the geocentric and heliocentric positions entered with the help of different-colored magnets. The most interesting discoveries can be made!

When the 90°- circle is used, the halfsums can be determined at the same time with the help of the calculation disc.

3. The Direction Circle. To find progressions for any given year, two K2 Form circles, one large, one small, are cut out. The same positions have been marked on both circles. By only moving the circles around to the solar arcs and years the progression for every age can be determined. The smaller circle is held in place and the larger one moved around. For an age of 30 years, the lower 0° mark is moved around to 30°.

To avoid cutting up the form with birth chart, the positions can be entered in the form in the outer 90° circle, the smaller circle laid on top and moved around. The result remains the same.

4. Working with the 45° Graphic Ephemerides. If nut and bolt and form are removed, the 45° ephemeris can be clamped in place, with a strong piece of paper slipped underneath to cover up the center hole, which would only be in the way when the lines are drawn.

Included with the workboard is a ruler with a side guide. If the form has been clamped exactly in place, the ruler only has to be

Fig. 4. Here the drawing device has been laid down along the top of the board to draw lines with the ruler through the form. To facilitate drawing, nut and bolt and peg can be removed, and magnets can be used to hold down the paper.

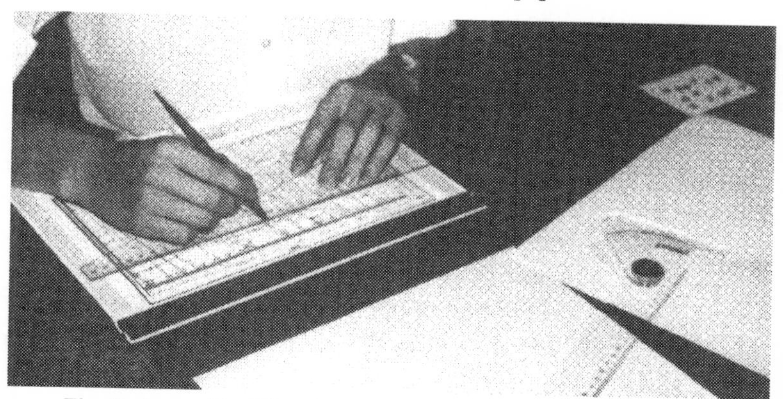

Fig. 5. A graphic 45°-ephemeris has been clamped in place and the simple ruler in use. The ruler only has to be shoved further along to draw the horizontal llines, one after the other.

shoved along the left side to achieve exact horizontal lines, the position lines, which intersect the planetary orbits. The ruler can also be used vertically to mark single days.

There is also another possibility of working. The positions of the cosmograms in question are drawn on transparent paper. This

Fig. 6. Once a solar arc direction has been drawn on the direction form the draw device is exactly adjusted and the parallel direction lines can be easily drawn..

is then clamped in together with the graphic ephemeris, care taken that the marking points or lines are aligned at 0° and 45°. In this way it is possible by laying down at once transparent diagrams for several persons to check for possible common experiences.

5. Comparing life diagrams, contact pictures, heredity constellations. Progressions can be noted down in the form of life diagrams according to the new method. The necessary forms are also available on transparent paper. It is therefore possible to lay the life diagrams of partners over one another and to clamp them in place. Now similar progressions at the same events in life can be seen.

If the cosmogram of a partner is also on transparent paper, this can also be included in the clamp. Here it is helpful to lay a blank piece of paper over the cosmogram and then to enter the positions from another cosmogram, taking care that each time the center point and zero point are marked precisely, so that the correct position can be found again. For quick analysis the magnets can of course be used for the partners.

Our form for heredity constellations (EKT 1) is also available on plain and transparent paper. All aspects and halfsums can be entered in these forms. By laying the transparent forms of a family one over the other, conformities can be swiftly ascertained. These forms are suited also for series analysis of vocational groups to work out conforming constellations.

The Versatile Workboard has manifold uses.

The simple workboard is made of cardboard with the usual surface for the K2 Form, nut and bolt, and calculation disc. It is not magnetized and has no clamp to aid in drawing the annual and life diagrams.

The pocket workboard is well-equipped and comes in a plastic case, and has small nut and bolt and calculation disc and short instructions for use. For this device you use the K1 Form with 9cm diameter.

An Infant Is Taken Ill

Until a child is able to speak the doctor is dependent upon external symptoms and his mechanical aids. A baby is not able to say where it hurts. It can only scream when a sensitive spot is touched. A cosmogram should not be expected to replace a medical diagnosis, but it can be of assistance.

Fig. 29 is the cosmogram of a girl born July 3, 1950, at 15 hours at lat. 54°N and long. 10°E.

For practical reasons, it is advisable on each occasion to set up one chart for keeping in one's record file, and a second one to be cut out for use with the dial. If a rapid survey is required, the indicator of the calculating disc is placed on the individual factors and midpoints; any aspects obtained are then written down as has been done in Fig. 29. A better, more comprehensive picture is obtained by setting up a structure picture, as has previously been explained. Those constellations which may indicate sickness have been underlined in Fig. 29. We note immediately the sickness significator Saturn/Neptune is tenanted by Mercury, Pluto and the Node. This indicates the possibility of long-lasting diseases being contracted. If the parents realize this they may take preventive measures right from the beginning.

Mars on Mercury/Neptune and Sun on Mars/Neptune = Uranus/ Neptune at worst indicate a nervous weakness, nerve paralysis, proneness to epidemics, lack of resistance, fits (spasms). Moon and Neptune on Saturn/Pluto can lead to poisoning in certain circumstances. Saturn in the different midpoints indicates disturbances in the fluid balance of the nervous system, in the muscles,

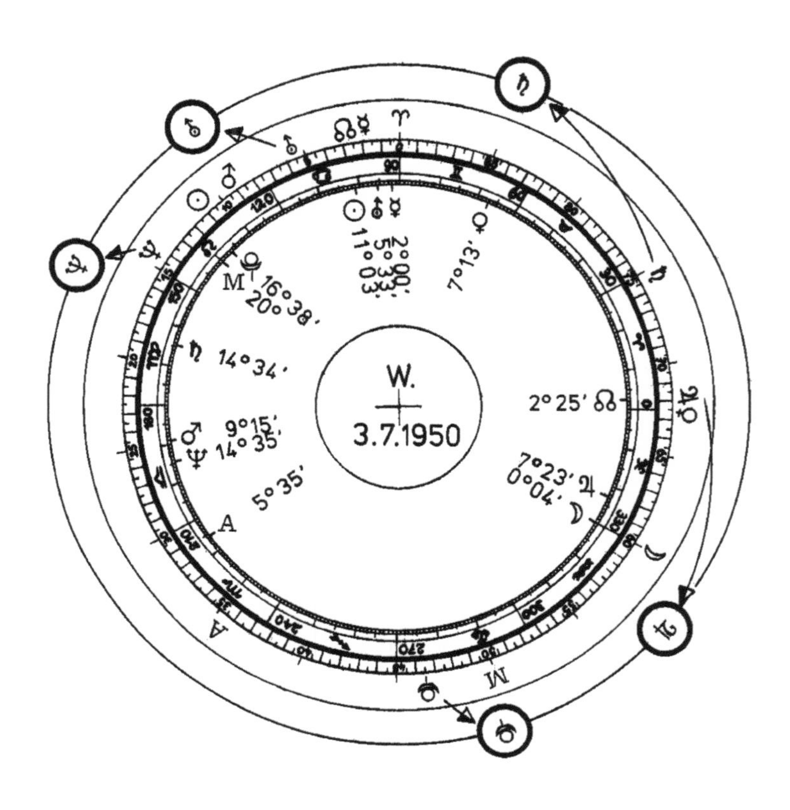

☿ □ ☊ = ⊖ = ♄/♆
♅ = M = ☿/♂ = ♂/☊ = ☉/☿
♂ □ ☉ = ☉/♅ = ☿/♆ = ☽/⊖
= ☽/M
☉ □ ♂ = ♂/♆ = ♅/♆
♆ = ☽ = ♄/⊖ = ♃/M = ♀/M
A = ☉/☽ = ♃/♅ = ♀/♅
♃ □ ♀ = ☽/♄ = ☉/A
♄ = ☽/☿ = ♂/M = ☉/M = ♆/⊖

Fig. 29

and in the relationship between the body and the ego-consciousness. A persistent diseases condition may develop.

The result of this brief and rough investigation, which can be checked in the CSI, is not pleasant. One can of course not yet say when these sicknesses as indicated are likely to appear. For this very reason, it is recommended to observe the infant's cosmogram and to move the magnet-planets daily according to the ephemeris. In this way, a picture of the infant's condition can be made up to a certain point. One will notice good progress under some configurations and under others interruptions in the development of the child. The greatest value should be placed in the slow moving planets. At the beginning of October, these take up the positions marked here by the symbols in the circles. The arrows represent the movement since the birthday. Jupiter was retrograde at that time, hence the arrow points in the opposite direction.

Observing the individual orbits closer, we note that the slow movers have not yet formed any aspect, with the exception of Jupiter retrograde just having passed over the Moon. According to our overall picture there is then a connection with Neptune and Saturn/Pluto, where under circumstances one may suspect the onset of a disease.

The more powerful transits only start developing in October. Pluto t at MC can indicate a big change or turn of events in the life. which is hardly imaginable with respect to such a small infant. Simultaneously, however, Uranus is also stimulated on various midpoints.

The essential point here is that Pluto t is still on the midpoint Saturn/Neptune, and this current configuration is shifting towards the MC.

Uranus t has reached the exact square to Mars; Mars, in the birth-chart, is on Sun/Uranus = Mercury/Neptune = Moon/Pluto = Moon/ MC. Let us read again the interpretations corresponding to these aspects, among others: nerve paralysis, proneness to infections (epidemics), lack of resistance, spasms (fits).

We have already determined that Saturn and Neptune are involved as their midpoint concurs with Pluto t and MC r = Uranus r. Let us now examine Neptune t in the axis Saturn/MC; we can deduce that, at the very least, setbacks in development are to be expected. Saturn t on the midpoint Saturn/Uranus also indicates some sort of crisis.

What in fact did happen? The child thrived for the first three months. We too determined that at that time no special transits were active. At the age of about three months a feverish infection was contracted. The proneness to epidemic diseases was previously indicated by Sun square Mars = Mars/Neptune. As at that time several cases of encephalitis had occurred in the village, treatment with sulphonamides was immediately given. This apparently cured the infection, but in the further development of the infant signs of a severe encephalitis were evident, with cerebral spasms and hemiplegia, which has been slightly regressing since 1956. At the age of 6, this child still could not speak, but understood everything. (One may also refer to this very same case given in the book *Die Jahreskurve*. In this presentation it is clearly obvious that the Jahreskurve (yearly curve) reached an unusual low at this time). In the CSI, on page 161 under Mars/Neptune, not only infectious diseases are indicated but also the possibility of paralysis. Here we do get a large number of exact correlations. We do not want to enter into a discussion, as to whether (through an understanding of the configurations) the child's illness might have been prevented; we are only concerned with the facts.

Those who possess the book *Die Jahreskurve* will find in example 2 the cosmogram of a child who has had to undergo a hernia operation at the age of 2 months. One will see within 7° of Neptune:

Saturn, Moon, Venus and, opposite, the two "operation-planets" Mars and Uranus. The disease which led to an operation was induced by the transit of Saturn over Venus, Shortly afterwards, Uranus t formed an angular relationship to Jupiter, which was followed by a very quick recovery.

Children Threatened Psychically

Parents and teachers cannot always be with the children in their charge. There are, however, times when children are in danger and constant supervision is necessary.

As one does not always know the exact birth-time (or does not wish to make special enquiries), an example where the birth-time is unknown follows. This case originates from a series of reports prepared for a university clinic; therefore, we may presume that the details are reliable.

On examination of the birth-chart of the little girl born July 30, 1943, our first impression is that she seems to be especially favored by fortune through the close conjunction of Jupiter, Sun, Pluto. Traditionally, the trine of Venus and Mars would promise good prospects for love relationships later on. However, the picture changes instantly, once we have transcribed the cosmogram to the 90° dial, and the individual factors are investigated. The most important configurations are reproduced in Fig. 30. Here, the unusually heavily tenanted midpoint Venus/Neptune strikes us at once. Let us note the most important interpretations:

Venus/Neptune
= Sun: romantic disposition, an erotic imagination, love-sickness.
= Jupiter: rich imagination, reveling in illusions, unreal or only apparent happiness in love.
= Saturn: pathological disposition with regard to the expression of love, love-sickness.
= Pluto: erotic aberrations caused through strong, unrequited love, tragic love, painful renunciation.

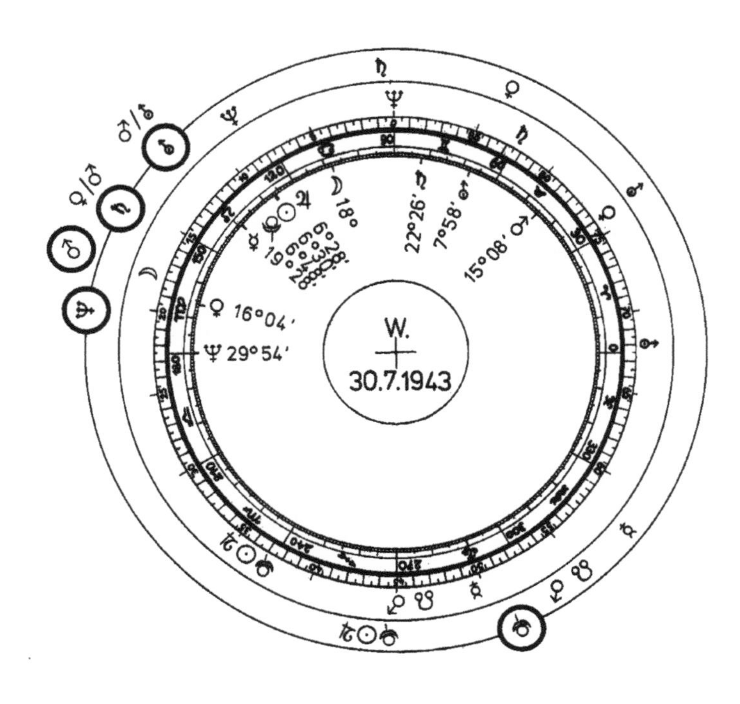

♆ = ♂
♄ = ♃ ☉ ⊖ = <u>♀/♆</u>
<u>♀ = ♄/♅</u>
♅ = ♂/♆
☿ = ☽/♄ ?

Fig. 30

Additionally we find:

Venus = Saturn/Uranus: tensions or stresses in a love relationship often leading to a separation.

Now, one may think that the purport of these configurations may only be noticeable later, when the girl is a little older. As has been proved by numerous examples in *Rapid and Reliable Diagnosis* such configurations become active when the individual factors of such a planetary picture are stimulated by solar arc directions. The distance between Uranus - Venus - Saturn - Neptune in the 90° circle is 6° - 8°. One would hardly expect this configuration to have effect at the age of 6 to 8 years. And yet this was just the case.

It was remarked in the case history that the parental farm was burnt down in 1951, which undoubtedly made a lasting impression on the child's mind, and that in the winter of 1951-52 she was sexually assaulted. In December 1953 it became necessary to place the child in the charge of the child welfare office; the following Spring the girl was admitted to a mental home. There was also a note to the effect that the illness must have commenced in winter of 1951-52, that is, after the rape.

The transiting planets may now be placed in position on the magnetic dial; we have taken the beginning of January. If we set the dial so that the indicator points to Venus and directed Uranus, then this position will coincide with the midpoint of Uranus t/Plu-to. The interpretation in the CSI (which applies to normal situations) reads: "a conquest in love." Well, it was no conquest in love, it was asexual assault, but it is quite possible that the child occupied herself with things normally reserved for a more mature age. Besides, the child is from a farming family. She might already have made observations on animals which fired her lively imagination. We do not know the exact circumstance and to avoid arriving at the wrong conclusions do not wish to speculate.

Looking at the transiting planets above left, this planetary configuration can by no means be called favorable. It is probable that Saturn or Neptune, the two sickness significators, are in connection with the girl's Moon. which would indicate a tendency towards psychiatric disorders.

Uranus t on Mars/Uranus may point to an injury. Important is the position of Saturn exactly on the midpoint Venus/Mars. The normal interpretation is: "inhibitions in love relationships, tendency towards extra-marital unions, pathological urges." Accordingly, these show the correspondence between the configurations and the happening. Moreover, Mars t passed over these points at that time.

However, one must not conclude that all children born on that day should have experienced similar fates. This cannot be the case, because children born on the same day all live in different circumstances which need not at all stimulate such a combination.

The next example concerns a youth born on July 21, 1941. For discretionary reasons, the place and time cannot be given (Fig. 31).

Firstly, it is interesting that the boy was born during an air-raid alert. One should note that Pluto lies in the meridian axis, which in the 90°-circle also makes a contact to Moon = Mars/Uranus. It is not unthinkable that the terror which the mother passed through at the moment of birth was imbedded in the child's subconscious mind. The position of the Sun on Uranus/Neptune makes the body sensitive and the mind impressionable. Mercury and Mars square could indicate a very lively and agile mentality, and through Mercury = Jupiter/Pluto and Jupiter/MC the native may get on well in life. Mercury and Mars on the midpoints Sun/Moon and Venus/Saturn points to special problems in love relationships. The same is indicated by Saturn = Venus/Uranus, while Saturn = Moon/Pluto = Moon/MC = Sun/Neptune are indicative of emotional experiences, a tendency to depression and illness. Only a few characteristics have been picked out.

If we set the larger disc of the dial at 15°, the solar arc corresponding to 15 years, we will find that Neptune s and Node s move over Mars r. In the 360°-circle it is an opposition. Therefore, the South Node is conjunct Mars.

We have a connection between Neptune, Node and Mars. Here we should mention that it is not necessary for one factor to be posited exactly on the midpoint of the other two; the essential fact is that the three factors form a particular relationship. There is no great difference between examining Mars = Neptune/Node or considering Node = Mars/Neptune. According to the CSI we get the

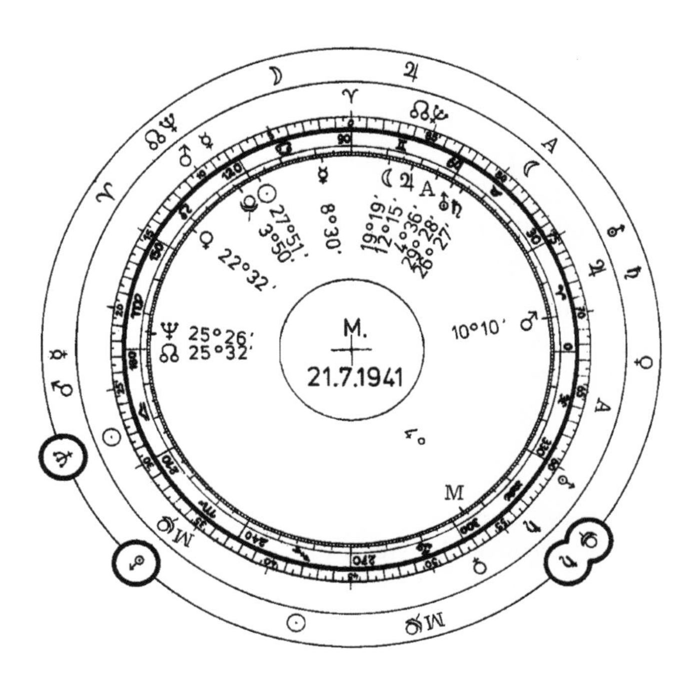

M = ⊖ ☽ ♃/♆ = ♃/☊ = ☿/♅ = ♂/♅
A = ♃/♄ = ☉/☿   ☉ = ♃ = ♅/♆
☿ = ♂ ☉/☽ = ♃/⊖ = ♃/M = ♀/♄
♀ = ☉/☽   ♂ = ☉/☽ = ♀/♄
♄ = ♀/♅ = ☽/⊖ = ☽/M = ☉/♆
♅ = ♀/A = ♆/⊖ = ♆/M = ⊖/☊ = ☊/M

Fig. 31

following interpretation:

Mars = Neptune/Node: disharmony when working or living together with others, inability to adapt oneself, disharmonious association, being together with sick people.

Node = Mars/Neptune: undermining of associations through lack of stability, unreliability, weakness of will or negative attitude, association with weak or sick people.

Because of Neptune s = Mars r on Venus/Saturn there is a possible danger that the 15 year old will have a peculiar sexual experience or be seduced.

An aspect of Mars and Neptune almost always pertains to weakness, to susceptibility to disease, and hence to a state conducive to any sort of influence, where the individual lacks the strength to resist or to assert himself.

With the magnetic dial at hand we can now insert the slow movers, otherwise we place another sheet of paper underneath and mark the positions of the transiting planets on it. We now determine that Neptune s = Mars is joined by Neptune t = Sun, indicating bad health.

Uranus t is in the same place with Pluto and the MC. This suggests a very exciting experience which in some way relates to the whole personality. As Moon r is in the same axis it could be an emotional experience. The midpoints Mercury/Uranus and Mars/Uranus could point to something very sudden or an accident.

Furthermore we find Saturn t in connection with Saturn r = Venus/ Uranus = Moon/Pluto = Moon/MC = Sun/Neptune. Wouldn't it be justified to deduce from this that an unpleasant erotic experience (Saturn = Venus/Uranus) will lead to psychic disturbances and depressions?

What in fact did happen was: the youth had to be admitted to hospital following a knee cartilage injury sustained in sporting activities. In our investigation we saw that the possibility of sickness (Neptune = Sun) and an accident (Uranus t = Pluto = MC + Mars/ Uranus, and so on) existed. In the two-bed ward was also an older man suffering from the same complaint. (Neptune/Node s; Mars: association with sick people.) One day in August 1956, the youth appeared unusually distracted. He was withdrawn and did not wish to communicate with anyone. Eventually he confided to his mother that he had been attacked by the sick man, strangled and sexually assaulted. The man had homosexual tendencies.

The author was unaware of this when the parents consulted him about their son. They only mentioned that their son showed no willpower and found it difficult to study. However, after the birth-chart had been set up, the main configurations were recognised. It was explained that the boy must be very emotionally sensitive, easily influenced without his having the strength to resist and that an emotional experience might lead to a passive attitude and possibly an illness. Only after that did the mother give the facts, as they have been related here.

These examples are intended to show that it is definitely possible to observe the development of children in the cosmogram and perhaps intervene at the right moment so as to prevent harm coming to them.

Difficulties at School

Many parents worry about their children when they are unable to keep up with the rest at school, or, after having done very well, suddenly fall back. These school-problems cannot be solved on a cosmic basis alone but it is possible to provide many useful pointers.

First the following questions have to be answered:

1. Do the trends shown in the cosmogram indicate alack of talent or do they point to a different talent?
2. Are the difficulties only temporary?
3. How many of the difficulties at school are due to the parents' attitude toward the child?

We already see from these questions that in order to judge a case correctly, psychological knowledge is absolutely essential. Those who do not possess it should not hesitate to consult a specialist.

The girl, born July 28, 1939, was causing her mother concern. as she showed no particular interest in anything, had failed her examinations for higher education, and was now ready to leave school without having the slightest idea of what to do next. (Fig. 32)

The birth-chart shows very many contradictions which are prominently indicated in the 90°-circle: the conglomeration of Mars, Saturn, Pluto, Node and Sun below left, and above right, Neptune, MC, Moon. Especially MC = Moon/Neptune shows a sensitive, easily hurt personality who would prefer to be lost in

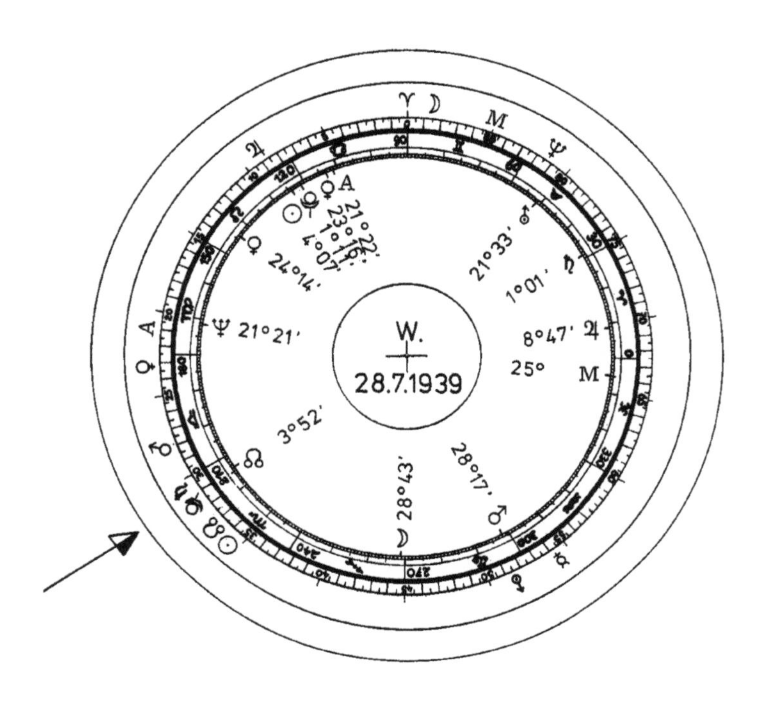

Fig. 32

thoughts and dreams. In contrast, the picture around the Sun and Saturn shows the hard reality, which does not permit dreams. The square of Sun and Saturn signifies a hampering influence on the whole development. Here it is particularly important to recognize the slow developer and not to force the child to a faster tempo for which she simply does not have the strength. As the Moon's Node joins this configuration, she is simply unable to communicate freely, partially from fear of being misunderstood or being ridiculed. The relationship between mother and daughter does not appear quite as it should be. With the previously mentioned tendencies the mother can hardly expect the child to be frank with her, but it is up to the mother to find the way to the child's soul.

Inhibited and slow developing children want to be "opened up" because they are unable to open up of their own accord. Besides, it is known that these children are tackling many problems within themselves. The point is whether or not they can solve them. Their ability to solve their problems successfully will decide whether or not they can develop into "full-blown" and successful individuals. Therefore, one must never see only the negative traits in such configurations. Sun square Saturn, for instance, is found in the nativity of the writer H. W. Geissler, who admitted to the author himself what difficulties he had had to overcome. He surmounted them and is now one of the best known novel writers in the German speaking world. The same configuration is present in the chart of the well-known actor Walter Giller, the American politician Bowles, and others. One must move away from the concept that individual aspects are "baddies" and others "goodies" as happens in traditional astrology. Such descriptions are simply misleading.

The girl has two brothers, who constantly get at her and ridicule her. Therefore, it is understandable that she is shy and inhibited. Here it should have been the duty of the parents to see to it, that the brothers behaved more gentlemanly towards their sister. How can such a child learn to succeed if things are made difficult even at home?

It came to light at an interview with the mother that the child does not take part in P.T. or any other kind of sporting activity. Therefore it was strongly advisable for the child to join a gymnastic group. Not only to learn to relax through exercises but also to open up in the company of her own age-group.

Through the position of Sun conjunct Pluto, the girl has undoubtedly the ability to succeed and make her presence felt, once she has overcome her feelings of inferiority, for which the parents are also partly to blame. The girl herself endeavored to achieve importance by playing much with younger children. She liked to spend a great deal of time with a large family, where she felt at home and was understood. She behaved more naturally to the mother of this family than towards her own mother, with whom the right contact just could not be made. Occupying herself with other children gave her growing motherly feelings in the puberty period a better outlet than in her own home.

As the lack of contact ability and her sensitive disposition might create difficulties in partnerships and in a possible marriage, we advised the mother to let her daughter train for some kind of profession. Children's nurse, kindergarten teacher or social worker were recommended as suitable.

The Choice of Occupation According to the Cosmogram

"Shall we carry on the game of wild imagination and give free rein to combination-mania? I cannot share the viewpoint of the purely aesthetical admirer of astrology, who does not wish to know anything about the experiments, even in limited psychological fields, of an astrological practice." These sentences already occur in the 1928 textbook *Berufsbegabung und Berufsschicksal —Astropsychologie der Berufsbegabung* (Vocational Talents & Fate-Astropsychology of Vocational Talents) by H. Frhr. von Klöckler (34). In this book, he also describes the Placidian House division as essentially incomplete, a method which the modern, advanced student can do without. Furthermore he considered it impossible to give "predictions as to a suitable vocation on the basis of stellar configurations alone" since "practically, there is no such thing as a Saturn, Jupiter or Mars occupation."

According to traditional astrology, Mars, for example, is the ruler of occupations such as that of the butcher, surgeon, the armed forces, blacksmiths etc. This summary alone shows that in this way one cannot arrive at a clear-cut result. Certainly, Mars is of importance in these occupations, but in each case in different configurations and it is these, not only Mars, that matter. Von Klockler considered it just as useless to put the onus on certain signs at MC and in the so-called occupation-house for any explanations with respect to a vocation. He also discarded the use of the so-called rulers and wrote at the end of his introduction: "It is self-explanatory that we shall not open to our readers' eyes the witches' cauldron of dispositors, rulers of decanates, antisciens, the earth horoscopes, etc. etc." It is regrettable that even in 1972 one is still coming across these astrological superstitions, when every clear-thinking person must realize that one cannot arrive at a true result with such practices.

This traditional astrological method has also been refuted by the very diligent and comprehensive work of the French psychologist Michel Gauquelin of the University of Paris *L'influence des astres* (The Influence of the heavenly bodies), Paris, 1955. (35).

Actually, Gauquelin's original intention had been to disclaim astrology. He cleared up numerous mistaken beliefs through research, but at the same time, he became so fascinated by the cosmo-terrestrial relationship that he carried on his investigations. Among other things, he investigated thousands of horoscopes with respect to the distribution of the individual heavenly bodies; starting from the Ascendant, he divided the "heavens" into 12 and also 18 areas. If the positions of the planets in certain areas or a certain distance from the Ascendant were decisive, then corresponding results would have to become apparent. Gauquelin counted his houses clockwise from the culminating point, in contrast to astrology's illogical numbering counterclockwise. Therefore, in the following survey the astrological house numbers are given in brackets. They do not correspond exactly, as Gauquelin worked with houses of equal size.

Of 676 members of the armed forces, 70 (the highest number) have the Sun in the 2nd (8th) and 12th (6th) houses. This is a little more than 10%. For Venus, the highest numbers are 74 and 76 in the llth (5th) and 12th (6th) houses. For Mars, who should have very special significance, the highest number is 70 in the 1st (7th) and 4th (10th) houses. This could perhaps be considered a confirmation of traditional astrological belief, as Mars would be expected to be most conspicuous near the AS or the MC, but we should have to allow an orb of 15°. Jupiter is 76 times m the 4th (10th) house, that is, about 1/9th of the investigated charts or about 11%.

Of 884 members of the clergy as a counterparts to the members of the armed forces, 109 have the Sun in the 12th (6th) house, i.e., in the "sickness-house" of traditional astrology. Mercury is 103 times in the 11th (5th), i.e., in the traditional "children's house". Venus is in the same place 99 times. Mars falls 93 times in the 3rd (9th) house. Accordingly, one could deduce a generous 11% are religious (9th) fighters (Mars). In 83 cases, Jupiter is in the 8th (2nd) house, the traditional "money house."

If other occupations are investigated in this manner, the results are no different. The traditional house-system, therefore, contradicts itself, if subjected to even the merest attempt at a scientific investigation. Who can take it upon himself to use rules, as demonstrated above, that prove to be correct only up to about 10 to 12 % of the time?

Therefore, it is surely better to rely on factors that are actually present and forget the traditional, superstitious ornamentations.

(For better understanding, reference can be made to the booklet *Hermes Trismegistos, Die Lehre der 12 Hauser oder Orte*, a special edition of *Kosmobiologie*, Ebertin-Verlag, 708 Aalen.)

If one wishes to consult the cosmogram in order to choose a vocation, one must firstly clearly understand that it is just not possible to read a particular occupation from a chart. One can only recognize certain abilities indicating the vocational areas. These limits have to be accepted right from the beginning.

As one of the most important discoveries of recent years we can point out in accordance with psychological principles, that it is necessary for a human being to be able to realize his aptitudes in some way or other. There are many cases, in which a person is forced to take up a particular occupation, resulting in life-long unhappiness and subsequent inability to achieve anything worthwhile, because it did not suit him.

One may recall that in some regions it has become traditional for the firstborn to become a priest regardless of having any ability for the priesthood or not. In other cases, the son had to carry on the family business, even if he did not want to.

The example at hand concerns the son of a man with an academic education. For reasons of discretion more detailed information is omitted. It is understandable that the parents would have been very happy, had the boy remained at school and done his final exam, and then had gone on to university, like his father. (Fig. 3 3)

Let us first endeavor to get some idea of the aptitudes and occupational indications which appear to be inherent in the various factors.

Sun: inclination for a secure and a leading position, for instance, civil servant.

Moon: inclination for social vocations, where the emotional qualities can be used, for instance, care of children and young people (teacher, psychologist etc.).

Mercury: good grasp or understanding of a subject, critical ability, dexterity and agility in expression and writing, aptitude for business and scientific vocations.

Venus: a sympathetic nature as well as sense of harmony, beauty, art give the foundation for interior designers, artists of all sorts, beauticians, etc.

Mars: will, determination, activity, understanding of technical and manual work are among the qualities needed for mechanics, technicians, engineers, athletes, fighters.

Jupiter: the position of this planet is of special importance for successful activity in any occupation.

Saturn: concentration, perseverance, constancy, depth are the basic qualities for vocations carried out in quiet seclusion and not in the limelight of the public eye, which is as suited for the philosopher as for the farmer or forester. Saturn is by no means only a hampering factor, but also leads to rich and deep experiences in life.

Uranus: interest in all that is new and advanced; revolt against every tutelage and limitation mark the reformer and inventor in the same way as, in the negative meaning, it marks the revolters and revolutionists.

Neptune: receptivity for all sorts of new ideas, as well as a rich imagination, and the sympathetic understanding of the nature of other people and things are of importance to the actor, writer, as well as to the pick-pocket and swindler.

Moon's Node: the ability to make contact is necessary for all occupations which are dependent on working together with other people or any type of work where influence has to be wielded.

This summary must not be taken as a set of rules to identify a vocation. After all, no occupation can be determined from the interpretation of any one planet. In each case, several tendencies will have to be correlated. To an engineer a combination of Mars and Uranus or Mars and Mercury are of importance. If he hopes to be successful, Jupiter must be well placed. For a military career, Mars is by no means the only important planet, there must also be talent for leadership, circumspection and organizing ability, etc. For a medical career, Sun, Jupiter and Mercury are often indicative. For a scholar, we frequently find a strong Mercury, often in connection with Saturn. This is only a very rough outline, which every reader can supplement by studying the CSI. The essential thing is how these various factors are related to others in the cosmogram.

For me, one glance at the cosmogram (Fig. 33) sufficed to show that this boy was unlikely to do well at school and was hardly likely to be suitable for any scientific career. I had already a Mercury-Neptune contact in many cosmograms of school children who failed in scientific subjects but showed talents in other directions. In any case, one should never tell any child that he has no talent, and thereby instill a feeling of inferiority in him, but one should explain to him that his talents lie elsewhere and that there is no reason at all why he should not do well in life, providing he develops and applies his real aptitudes.

Where can we find an indication of aptitudes? We cannot do without looking up the most important configurations. (Those wishing to act in an advisory capacity in this field should most certainly make use of the various psychological tests.

The position of the MC indicates an optimistic outlook, adaptability, love of change (Jupiter/Uranus), popularity, perhaps artistic aptitudes (Venus/Jupiter), development of ego-consciousness, a powerful and purposeful nature (Moon/Mars), self-confidence, perseverance, ambition (Mars/Pluto).

From the position of the Sun we deduce: intellectual ability, realistic thinking, connections with the public (Moon/Mercury) impressionability (Neptune/Pluto) commanding respect (Pluto/AS), creative power, love of enterprise, organizing ability (Mars/Jupiter) love of being in the limelight, vanity (Venus/MC), unrest, mobility, lack of self-control (MC/Uranus).

Moon in connection with Jupiter points to an exaggerated emotional life, wavering between fanatical striving for the attainment of desired objectives and soft-hearted sentimentality, and on Mars/Saturn, lack of willpower, occasional despondency, illness, and also brutality and ruthlessness.

The Ascendant has connection with the previously mentioned Mercury-Neptune conjunction, giving it special significance in this cosmogram. The AS and MC always strike the keynote, and whose aspects to other factors may be of significance for the whole life.

Let us analyze in more detail:

Jupiter/Node = AS: the ability to come into personal contact with other people quickly through a pleasant and sympathetic disposition, harmonious relationship with the environment.

= Mercury: to cultivate exchange of thought with others, to organise associations or unions between people, joint successes, good co-operation.

= Neptune: emotional inhibitions in partnerships, indecision or vacillation, instability, unreliability.

Moon/MC = AS: emotional attitude to one's environment, comprehension of other people's emotional needs.

= Mercury; the emotions influence the thought-process.

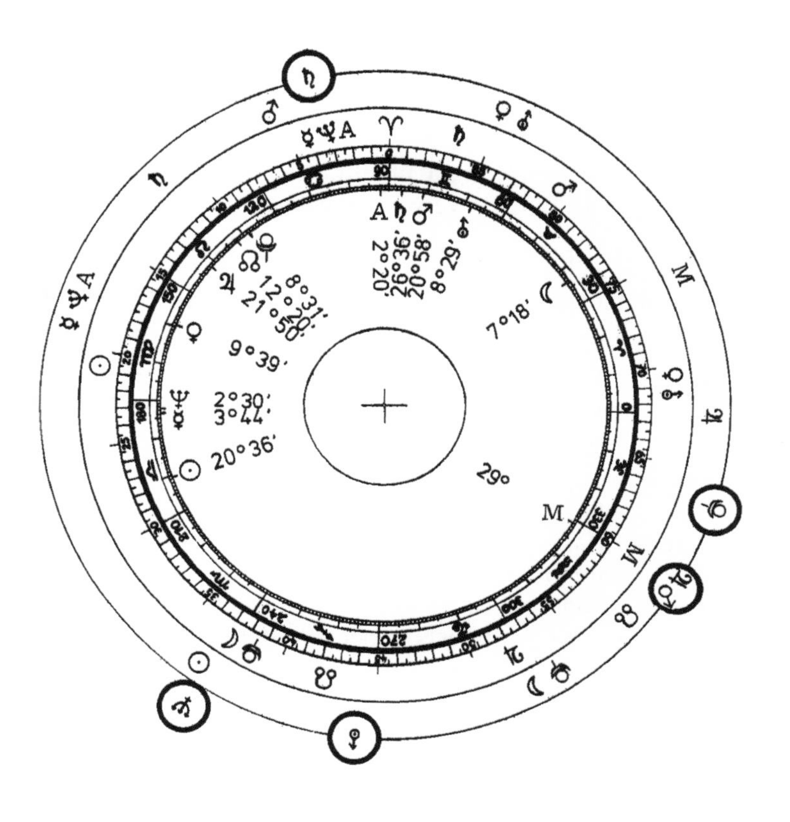

M = ♃/♅ = ♀/♃ = ☽/♂ = ♂/⊖
☉ = ☽/☿ = ♆/⊖ = ⊖/A = ♂/♃ = ♀/M = ♅/M
☽ □ ⊖ = ♂/♄
☿ = ♆ = A = ♃/☊ = ☽/M = ⊖/M
♀ = ♅ = ♃/♄ = ☿/☊ = ♆/☊
♂ = ♀/A = ♀/♆ = ☿/♅ = ♅/♆ = ☉/♃
♃ = ☊/M = ☉/♂
♄ = ♂/♆ = ♂/A = ☿/♂ = ☊

Fig. 33

= Neptune: deceptive emotional ideas or pictures; going astray psychically.

Pluto/MC = AS: the attainment of importance and recognition under any circumstances.

= Mercury: great intelligence, success in the sphere of science, to act with powers of suggestion.

= Neptune: peculiar objectives in life, rich imagination.

From the remaining constellations we select a few which appear to be of importance:

Mercury/Uranus = Mars: quick grasp of a situation, courage, determination, personal success. Sun/Jupiter = Mars: zeal, eagerness, success.

Mars/AS = Node: companionableness, working for the community.

Mercury/Mars = Node: the realization of thoughts in association with others.

Mercury/Node = Venus: seeking association with people having the same interests, especially in the artistic field.

Mercury/Node = Uranus: to get stimulating ideas through other people, the formulation of new ideas jointly with others.

These various individual interpretations give us the following indications for a choice of occupation:

A scientific vocation is not suitable. The desire to work, ambition and ability to succeed are present, but any regular activity which demands patience and perseverance deserves less consideration; the job should rather provide variety. As there are some indications for unreliability, but for adaptability as well, it appears that a job within a working association is to be preferred, in order to realise plans and objects jointly with others. This would also provide the possibility to understand others emotionally and influence them accordingly.

Now for the facts: already during the first school years, this child's nativity was comprehensively investigated. In 1958, the cosmo-psychogram was set up and in the light of this the vocational problem was discussed. This boy just did not wish to remain at school any longer. He very much wanted to become a photographer and, if possible, work in the film industry. The parents realized that coercion would be useless. They got in touch with a film studio, and now the author was asked when the most favorable time was for an interview, to take place some time between the end of January and the beginning of March 1959, if possible on a Friday. His father wrote: "So much of his future life depends on this introduction and interview, as he still absolutely refuses to sit at a school desk for yet another year."

In Fig. 33, the solar-arc directions show Moon s = Jupiter, which could bring about a happy turn of events for the boy. However, the transiting planets can in no way be considered favourable. We quote from the carbon copy of the letter in our files:

"The slow moving Jupiter in square to the MC, due on the 10th of February appears to be important. In addition, Mars/Sun, Venus and Mercury are forming an aspect to the MC, which, of course, indicates the ego-conscious drive. (In our Fig. 33 only Mars t and Jupiter t have been entered to give a clearer overall picture.

"The approximate opposition of Neptune and Moon on the 7th should preferably be over, and perhaps also Saturn square Mercury on the 9th. On the other hand. the Jupiter position should be exploited at all costs, because we have Jupiter = MC = Mars/Pluto = Jupiter/Uranus t: consciousness of objective, organising talent, unusual success, powers to succeed. (Please note the importance of evaluating the cosmic condition of the transiting planets!) Jupiter is also trine to your own Jupiter (in the father's cosmogram) and approaching the trine to the MC, which, however, does not become exact. In spite of the Saturn position, I would consider the 9th of February as the best day, because Sun trine Mars and Sun trine Sun allow for an increased productivity, in case some sort of test or exam has to be taken. On the 10th, Sun opposition Jupiter is due, joined by Mars square MC; Mars transits often are active in advance. On February 9th, Monday, we have therefore 'concentrated energy' in operation, as is necessary here. Friday the 6th comes too much under Moon opposition Neptune, Friday the 13th is somewhat 'flat,' on the 20th there is not much doing either. Therefore, I recommend the 9th or the 10th of February for the interview."

On February 20, the father replied: "On the 9th of February, as you suggested, we presented ourselves with our son. For the interview I selected the Jupiter-Mars opposition at 29° Scorpio as Ascendant. (Obviously, the father had also cast the cosmogram for the moment of introduction.) Our son has been accepted and the hoped for success achieved. . . ."

We consider this detailed discussion of this case justified by the vital importance of the question of choosing a vocation.

Vocational Fate and Success

Something about vocational development can only be predicted when the general background, that is the circumstances at home and the up-to-date occupational history are known. The general conditions prevailing at the time will also have to be considered. because for very many people the occupational vicissitude is dependent on economic, political conditions, and other factors. We only have to recall the fate of many businessmen at the time of inflation following the First World War, the years of unemployment in the early thirties, after 1933 (in Germany) the numerous dismissals of civil servants because they belonged to the wrong political party and simultaneously the ascent of many of the unemployed in the (Nazi) Party, the difficulties afflicting many after the Second World War through denazification and the ascent of those who had been expelled in the third Reich. Even at this present time the prayerbook is in some cases a more important passport to success than the show of actual experience and knowledge.

It is not so much a matter of what kind of obstacles the young person is confronted with, but how he masters them, the way he resolves conflicts with the parental home and with himself, and the way financial difficulties are tackled. The road to professional success is by no means dependent on the parents' help, but on the young person's early appreciation of the fact that he or she has to unfold his own initiative and to succeed under his own power.

Some indications of hampering obstacles may well be discovered in a cosmogram, but one can only very rarely, without further clues, recognise connections as to whether they will be overcome or whether perhaps an inferiority complex or ill health will develop before the vocational goal has been achieved.

Contrary to astrological tradition, one has to get away from two erroneous assertions:

1. Vocational fate and success are not dependent on the 10th house or the "occupation" house. It is indeed significant which planets and what kind of relationship the MC has with other factors, but not the positioning of particular planets in a certain sector of the zodiac circle. If statistical proof of this statement is required one should read *L'influence des astres* by Michel Gauquelin, Paris 1955, in which the various house-positions of the planets are investigated with respect to various groups of occupations.

2. It is absurd to regard certain angular relationships (square, opposition) as unfavourable and other (trine and sextile) as favourable, without taking "the nature of the planets" into account. In addition to the numerous examples shown in *Kosmobiologie* and in the *Kosmische Beobachter* we will later on be giving various examples in which particularly the squares and oppositions brought success.

It has been confirmed time and again that recognition, promotion and financial success correlate to certain Jupiter constellations formed by transits as well as by directions. Pluto often has a hand in unusual achievements. Sudden changes and adjustments are the result of combinations with Uranus. Special accomplishments through will-power correlate mostly with an angular relationship to Mars. Aspects alone are not decisive, the inclusion of the midpoints is always necessary.

Let us now study various vocational careers with the aid of the 90°-dial: A male birth on July 10, 1883, about 11 p.m. in Ernsdorf Kreutz-tal in Siegerland. (Fig. 34).

Looking at the birth chart, we find no planets near the MC, instead they are opposite in the "depth of heaven" around the 1C. It is true that Jupiter is conjunct the Sun, which may indicate success, but Saturn near Mars and Pluto points to an inhibited personality,

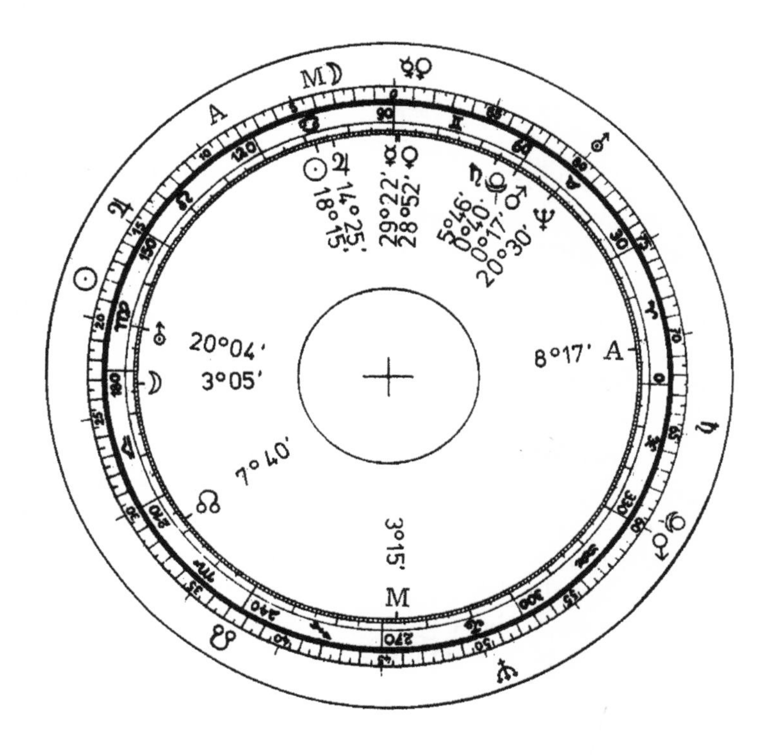

Fig. 34 Dr. Friedrich Flick

who is not able to make full use of his energy. Perhaps Sun sextile Uranus may be considered favourable.

When we examine that 90°-circle and set up the structure picture, one configuration impresses particularly: Jupiter = Mars = Pluto.

In the inner circle, Jupiter is semisquare to Mars and Pluto. (Under no circumstances should one think "only" a semi-square, because we may consider squares, opposition, trines, semi-squares and sesquiquadrates as being of equal value.)

"Consciousness of one's objective, the ability to organise, the right use of one's energy, the attainment of unusual successes, the enjoyment of one's freedom, " states the CSI. This constellation also falls on the midpoints Sun/AS and Uranus/Node, where it gains in importance in aspecting two "personal points" the Sun and AS.

If this truly is an essential configuration in the cosmogram, it would have to play a part when stimulated by directions and/or transits. Firstly, it is of importance that Jupiter is not retrograde but moves towards the Sun. The progressive Jupiter (1 day = 1 year of life) reaches 18°19' Cancer = Sun r on July 28, 1883, that is, at the age of 18. This is the time when one prepares for life at school. Under these constellation one is likely to take home good school-reports.

The solar-arc directions are measured on the dial with the calculating disc. The distance from Uranus to Jupiter (= Mars = Pluto) is about 24°, corresponding to ca. 1907. The distance from the Sun to Uranus is about 28°. According to the ephemeris the solar-arc is slightly smaller than the number of years, therefore, this direction becomes due at about 30 years of age, in 1913. When we place the indicator on Mars and Pluto, the difference to Mercury and Venus is about 29°, that is an age of slightly over 30. Significant is the time when the factors of the Jupiter - Mars - Pluto configurations inter-stimulate themselves, which may happen around the 45th year. By reason of the smaller solar-arc, one may decide on the 48th year of life, around 1931.

It is now necessary to determine if the results calculated so far really apply. We are looking at the chart of one of Germany's most successful industrialists, Dr. h.c. Dr. ing.e.h. Friedrich Flick. He was the son of a farmer who also dealt in mining struts. He went to the Handelshochschule (school of economics), graduated and became Diplomkaufmann (merchant with university degree). In 1907, at the early age of 24, he was granted power of attorney at the Bremen foundry (Uranus s = Jupiter = Mars = Pluto). In 1913, a fortunate turn of events occurred by his becoming a member of the board of directors of a steelworks in Menden and Schwerte (Uranus s = Sun, Mars = Pluto = Jupiter s = Mercury). The

Sun-Uranus contact correlated with an invention in which furnaces are fed with steel-shavings instead of ore. In 1915, this method was adopted by the Charlottenhutte (steelworks) in Niederschel-den, which invited F.F. to become its director.

In the years around 1931, Jupiter s reached the square to Mars and Pluto, and Mars with Pluto the conjunction to Jupiter. At this time of world economic depression he sold the majority share holdings of the Gelsenkirchner Bergwerke A.G. and with the proceeds founded the Mitteldeutschen Stahlwerke (steelworks), which rapidly grew enormously by taking over other factories. At the same time, he pursued his objective of making the Friedrich Flick KG a purely family concern, which he managed to do by 1934. In the following years he retired from public life, but wielded an important influence in the German armament industry and brought the mining companies of occupied Europe under his control.

Now, as we all know, a cosmogram does not only consist of favorable configurations. The Sun is in the axis of Mars, Pluto/ Saturn, which is not favourable, and Neptune in Saturn/Node could lead him into an unpleasant situation. Neptune s = Sun became exact in the first year of his internment in the Landsberger Kriegs-verbrechergefangnis (prison for war criminals) from which he was prematurely released in 1950. Although he lost almost 75% of his former possessions through demolition and dispossession and had to sell all his properties in the Ruhr, he nevertheless managed to rebuild the Flick concern in the following years, again taking part in numerous companies. It is impossible to mention all the known interests on one printed page; here are some: Daimler-Benz with 72 mills., Monopol-Bergbau with 40 mills., Auto-Union with 12 mills., Maximilians Hutte with 60 mill. DM and so on. Moreover, each of these companies controls further subsidiary companies.

This should be demonstration enough of the correlation between the success configurations and the various significant events triggered. Had one examined this cosmogram according to the housesystems Of traditional astrology, this successful personality would have been marked by Neptune on the cusp of the 2nd house (money, wealth) and this house tenanted by Mars, Pluto and Saturn, from which one is more likely to deduce financial difficulties or at least wrong speculations.

Another unusual successful personality is the American hotelier Conrad N. Hilton, who according to privately obtained information from the USA is said to have been born on December 25, 1887 at 5.20 a.m. in San Antonio (Fig. 35).

His father was very enterprising: He kept a store, also rented out stabling for horses and let rooms to transit travellers, became post-master and later a garage proprietor and in that capacity entered the banking business. After having finished with school and studies, C.N. Hilton worked for his father, ran a small private hotel and simultaneously worked in the bank. In 1913, father and son founded a bank, C. N. Hilton became cashier, but after only two years he was made president and part-owner of his father's other businesses. After some political activity and taking part in the First World War, C.N. Hilton tried resuming his banking business. Failing in this, he quickly decided to enter the hotel-business. His business activities proceeded normally and up to the time of the Second World War nobody could suspect that within a decade C.N. Hilton would rise to become the most powerful hotel-industrialist in the world. This development commenced in 1946. All the hotels, often distinguished by very special features, are spread throughout the world's capitals and count more than 45,000 rooms.

The birth-chart is probably correct, since MC, Mercury and Saturn are (in the 90°-circle) in the axis of Sun/Pluto and on Mars/ Jupiter and in a negative sense also on Mars/Neptune. From this we may deduce the following:

Sun/Pluto

= MC: striving for power, consciousness of goal, qualities of leadership.

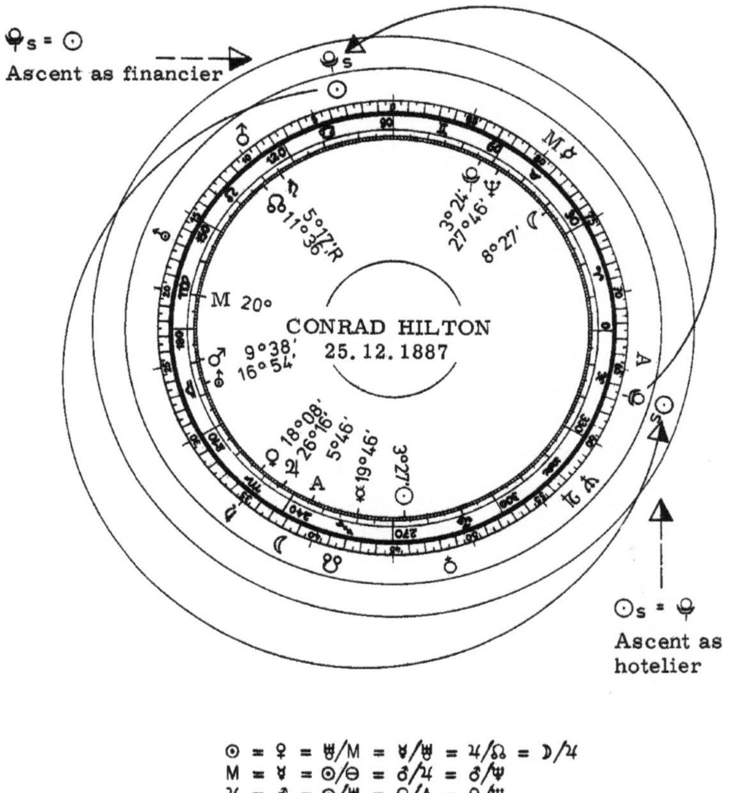

Fig. 35 Conrad Hilton

= Mercury: aspiring to intellectual supremacy, prudence, organising talent, consciousness of aim or objective, restless creative activity, a speaker with suggestive powers.
= Saturn: ruthless overcoming of obstacles and difficulties.

The Sun is also in a very strong position: the Sun is = Venus = Uranus/MC = Mercury/Uranus = Jupiter/Node = Moon/Jupiter, where especially the grasp of situations, the readiness for action, but also good cooperation and a social attitude are expressed.

The Pluto-Uranus contact indicates the revolutionary who wants to create and pioneer something new, all this in an area serving the comforts of life equally as much as occupational matters, and which maybe dedicated to Mercury as well as to Venus. Pluto lies in the axis of Mercury/Venus and Venus/MC, this again expresses a forceful, creative power. The progressive mind and the success in new ventures is shown in Mars = Jupiter = Sun/Uranus.

In the course of this life we have two decisive moments for the commencement of a successful development around the 28th year of life, when C. N. Hilton became president of the bank and his father's partner, and in the 59th year when the enormous hotel-concern began to develop.

It has been pointed out several times before that important planetary pictures stimulate themselves, in as far as one factor reaches another and vice-versa. This is a case in point. The ascent of the financier correlates with Pluto s = Sun and the hotel success to Sun s = Pluto.

Around 1920 he experienced a failure when he could not manage to expand his banking business further. At the age of 32, Sun s reaches the opposition of Saturn, indicating frustrations in his development.

A revolutionary in the grocery trade was the Swiss businessman Gottlieb Duttweiler, born August 15, 1888, about noon in Zurich. He introduced the mobile shop, serving a district at a time, achieved a large turnover with a small profit-margin, guaranteed fresh goods through date stamping, dispensed with excessive advertising, delivered at an exact price for odd weights and stocked only a small selection of quality goods. In 1925 he built up the Migros A. G. under great difficulties and animosity. (Fig.36)

In order to give as many examples as possible, some cosmograms have only been reproduced in the 90°- circle with their essential configurations to facilitate comparison. The most

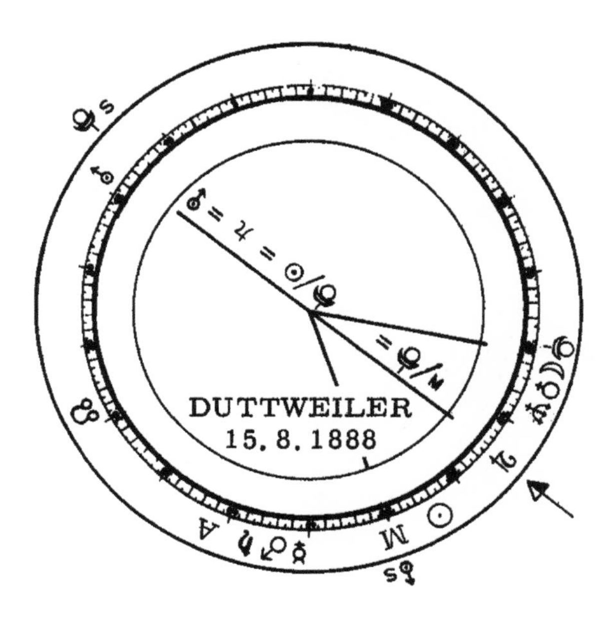

Fig. 36

important factors are: Sun = MC in Leo - 90 - Jupiter, Mars = AS, Uranus = Moon/ Jupiter = Sun/Pluto in contrast to Saturn - 90 - AS, Saturn = Mercury.

At the time of the establishment of the Migros A.G., the solar-arc was not quite 36°. Uranus s = MC indicates the revolutionary act, the introduction of a new sales technique. Pluto s = Uranus = Jupiter = Pluto/MC etc. led to the success of the enterprise in spite of the difficulties. In 1959, Duttweiler achieved a turnover of 760 million Swiss francs.

Two characteristic examples of a successful re-construction of business after the Second World War are Dr. Fritz Berg and Max Grundig.

Dr. Fritz Berg, born August 27, 1901, son of the owner of a factory manufacturing spokes for prams, bicycles and motorcycles,

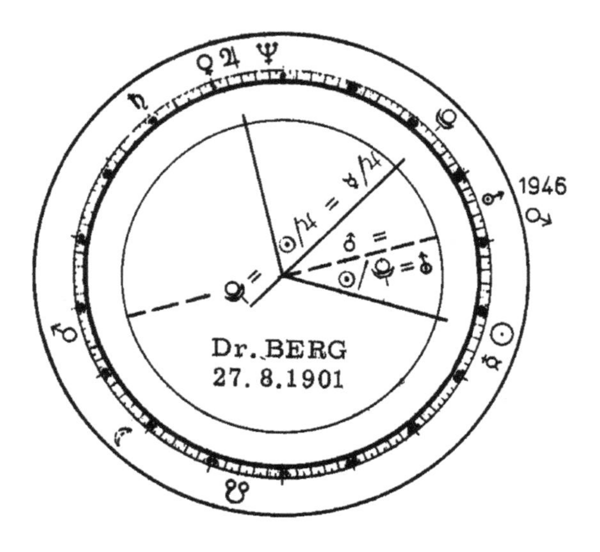

Fig. 37

cars and, later, springs for mattresses etc. Dr. Berg joined his father's firm in 1928 as head clerk, became part-owner in 1934 and after his father's death in 1940, sole owner. Through the war he lost the branches in East Germany and had to re-build his destroyed factory. He not only managed to reconstruct and enlarge his factory, but also gained general recognition through his organising ability, with the result that he was first elected chairman of his industrial organization and president of the South Westphalian Chamber of Commerce and Industry. In the following years numerous offices were added. In 1955, he was awarded the Bundesverdienstkreuz mit Stern und Schulterband (highest Federal award for achievement) and at present, he is taking an important part in German and international trade organizations. (Fig. 37).

In Fig. 37, we instantly spot Pluto = Jupiter/Sun and also Mars and Uranus on Sun/Pluto. About 1946, Mars s joined Uranus = Mars = Sun/Pluto, which the CSI interprets as: the desire to attain

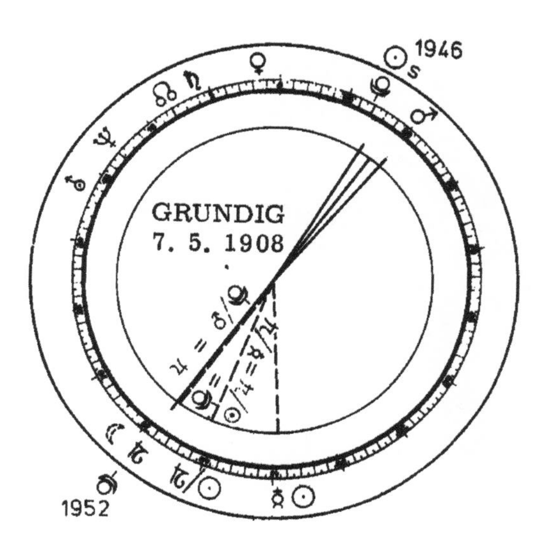

Fig. 38

record achievements, the tendency to work to the point of collapse. Here then we have a configuration indicating the efforts needed for a re-building program. When Mars s joined Pluto (= Sun/Jupiter) Dr. BERG was awarded the Bundesverdienstkreuz.

We find essentially similar constellations as Dr. berg's in Mr. Grundig's chart, that is Pluto = Sun/Jupiter = Mercury/Jupiter, where however a wider orb will have to be accepted. On the other hand, Jupiter is also on Mars/Pluto as in Dr. Flick's case and with a somewhat larger orb as in Herrn Duttweiler's as well (Fig.38).

Max Grundig was born May 7, 1908 in Nuremberg. From the beginning of radio, radio was his hobby, and later he opened a small radio shop. In 1946, with laboriously scrounged materials, he commenced building a small radio factory, at a time when the rest of the German radio industry was still in the doldrums and showed no initiative. He set about developing his enterprise, which in 1961 employed about 30,000 workers. Up to 1961, 10 million radio sets and 1 million television sets had been made.

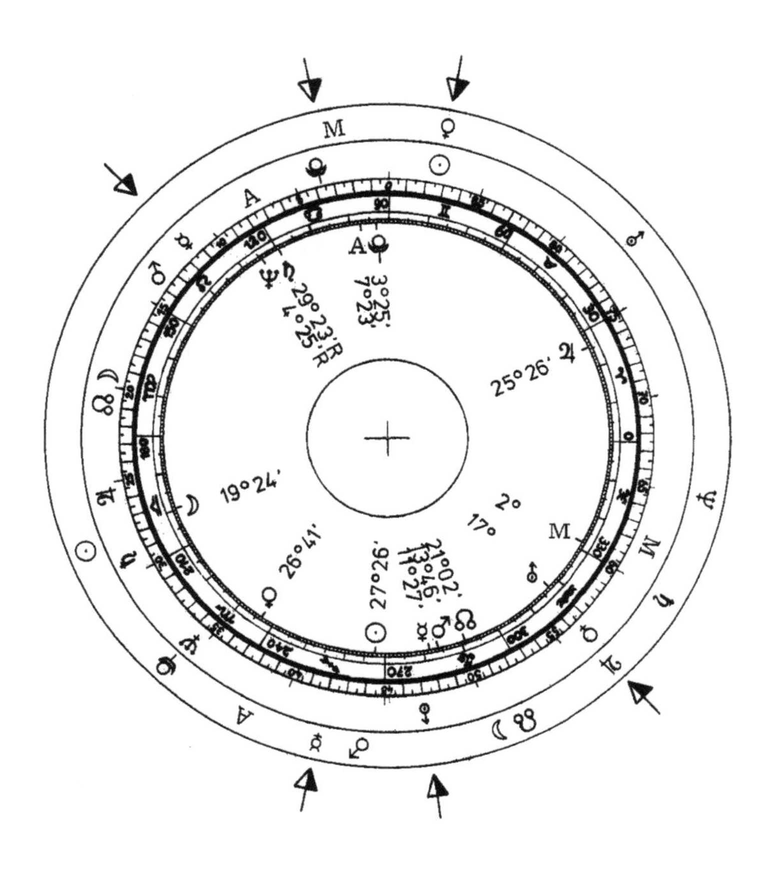

M
A
3°25'
7°23'
29°23'R
4°25'R
25°26'
19°24'
2°
17°
M
26°41'
27°26'
21°02'
13°46'
11°27'
A
M

♃ = ♅/⊖ = ♂/♆ =
M = ☽/♂ = ☿/☊ = ♂/☋ = ♄/⊖
☉ = ☊/M = ♀/♃
⊖ = ☉/☿ = ♆/M = ♅
☿ = ☽/⊖ = ☉/♃ = ♀ (= ♂)
♂ = ⊖/☋ = ☽/A = ☉/♄
☽ = ♂/♃ = ♆/⊖

Fig. 39

Here, too, we find the effect of the success configurations. In 1946, Sun s reached the natal Pluto (= Sun/Jupiter). In 1952, Grundig was awarded the Bundesverdienstkreuz, after the millionth radio had been produced and that was when Pluto s reached Jupiter.

The various examples in which only the day and not the time of birth are known prove that even on the basis of this simple framework the success configurations can be recognised. On no account should it be overlooked that it is absolutely essential to know the course of development up to date, the education, the environment and circumstances of the family background, and so on, so that these basic facts maybe combined with the cosmic configurations.

In scientific vocations, Elisabeth Noelle- Neumann holds a special position as a journalist and social research worker. As a foreign student in the USA, she studied and learned about opinions and mass-research and in 1946-47 with a very small team founded the Institut für Demoskopie, Gesellschaft zum Studium der offentlichen Meinung m.b.H. (Institute of Public Opinion and Society for Public Opinion Research Ltd.) in Allensbach. This company quickly became one of the most important instruments to politicians, industry, advertising and economy for the investigation of public opinion and influencing the people. (Fig. 39)

When investigating occupational matters, three points should be distinguished:

1. Which character qualities favor what vocational direction, for instance: independent or in employment, the suitability for a career in office work or in a profession. One has also to decide whether qualities of leadership are evident or if a subordinate position is to be taken into consideration.

2. In what type of occupation may these qualities best be used and in what type of activity may the person concerned find satisfaction.

3. What possibilities of success are inherent in the birth chart and when could they be materialised.

Re 1. in the example before us the following configurations may be selected:

MC = Moon/Mars: a powerful and purposeful nature.
MC = Moon/Mercury: independent thought, forming one's own opinions.
MC = Mars/Node: adaptability to a community; good cooperation.
Sun = Node/MC: clubbing together on account of shared interests.
Moon = Mars/Jupiter: intuitively making the right decisions.

This summary shows qualities for an independent occupation as well as for possibilities of cooperating with others.

Re 2. one will pay most particular attention to the positions of Mercury and Mars (thought and action):

Mercury = Moon/Pluto: the ability to influence a large circle through speeches or writings, the pursuit of far-reaching plans and ideas with great zeal.
Mercury = Sun/Jupiter: success through thinking, speaking and acting.
Mars = Pluto/Node: the desire to make others amenable to one's own wishes. (As primarily the interpretations as given in the CSI are used, these have been stated here, even if not quite relevant.)
Pluto = Sun/Mercury: suggestively influencing others.
Uranus = Sun/Mercury: a flair for technical sciences, organisation and reforms.

These constellations indicate very plainly the influence exerted on many people by speeches and writings, therefore pointing to a journalistic organising activity.

Success in connection with point 3) corresponds to planetary configurations composed mainly of Sun, Mars, Jupiter, and Pluto in positive relationship:

Jupiter = Uranus/Pluto: to achieve immense successes.
Mercury = Sun/Jupiter: see 2)
Moon = Mars/Jupiter: successful woman.

It is of course unavoidable that many configurations apply to more than one of the different points.

This public opinion expert established her business at the age of about 30. Let us move the various positions correspondingly, by a solar-arc of about 30°, then the MC is moving towards Pluto, which is on Sun/Mercury. This may be interpreted:

"I (MC) have far-reaching plans and am concerned with the influe-encing of the masses and the taking of polls (Pluto = Sun/Mercury) for the formation of an opinion (MC = Moon/Mercury)."

Jupiter s, very important for a good beginning, is, at the position of Venus r and opposite Mercury = Sun/Jupiter = Moon/Pluto. Jupiter, therefore, triggers the success corresponding to the vocational tendencies inherent in this personality (see point 2). The axis Mercury/Venus s is on Sun = Node/MC, thus confirming the agreement of the inherent tendencies with the occupational activity (CSI 1097).

Looking at the cosmogram of Karl Jaspers, one can hardly believe that this is the chart of a philosopher who is one of the most important thinkers of the present time. Of course, Sun in Pisces should indicate contemplation, as is apt for a philosopher; but how many people have the Sun in this sign without showing the slightest inclination towards philosophy. Moon conjunct Uranus is said to correspond to unrest, Mars square Neptune is considered disadvantageous for the physical as well as mental constitution. Where now is the configuration pointing to intellectual greatness and to the man's success? Would Mars trine Jupiter apply? To get a clearer answer, we shall have to take a closer look at the individual constellations (Fig. 40).

In the 90°-circle we see the Sun as midpoint, between two complexes: Uranus - Moon - Jupiter and Mars - Node - Neptune. This may be interpreted as follows: creative power, spirit of enterprise, organising talent, pride, sense of honour, success (Mars/Jupiter), perseverance, striving towards independence, consciousness of

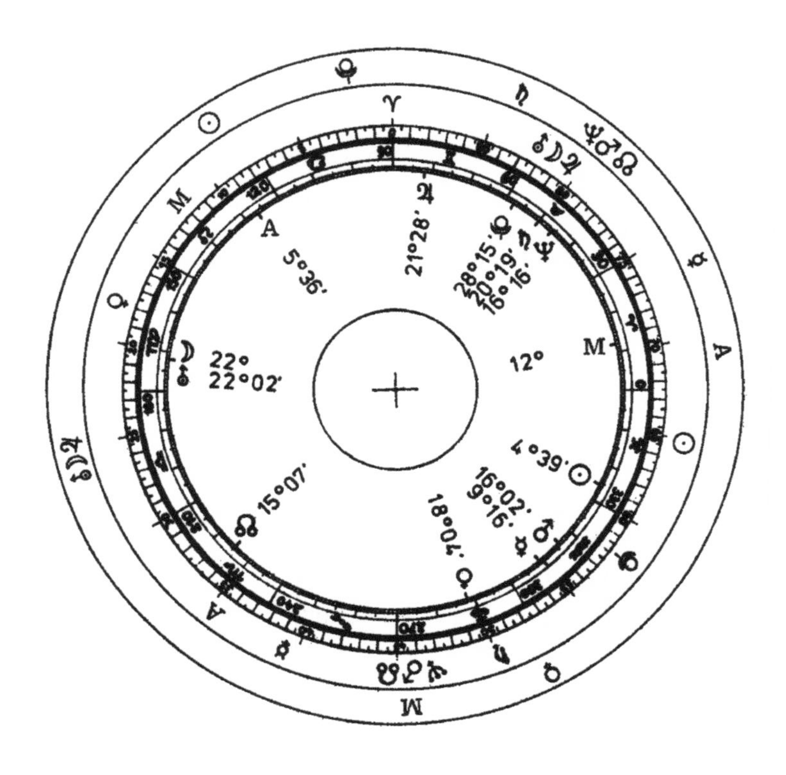

♃ = ☽ = ♅ = A = ☉/M = ☿/A
M = ⊖ = ☉/♄
☿ = ☉/M = ♀/⊖ = ☊/A
☊ = ♂ = ♆ = ☿/♄
☉ = ♅☽♃/☊♂♆

Fig. 40 Prof. Dr. Karl Jaspers

goal (Moon/Mars), capable of sudden action and extra-effort (Mars/Uranus), sensitive body (Uranus/Neptune), excitability (Uranus/Node), good fellowship, social conscience (Jupiter/ Node), speculation (Jupiter/Neptune), susceptible to impressions (Moon/Neptune), spiritual attitude to others (Moon/Node).

This summary shows us that these planetary configurations may be viewed positively, because mainly qualities of the will emerge which are essential to advance in life.

Interpreting the individual complexes, we get the following answers: Jupiter = Moon = Uranus = Sun/MC = Mercury/AS, this is a configuration containing all the personal points and is therefore likely to be of particular importance. A positive inner life, a social conscience (Moon = Jupiter), emotional tensions, manifestation of subconscious forces, self-willedness, striving towards an objective, the pursuit of one's own convictions (Moon = Uranus), optimism, thirst for knowledge, interest in philosophy of life (Jupiter = Uranus), to attain one's objectives through a positive outlook (Sun/MC = Jupiter), a restless intellect causing changes in one's objectives (Sun/MC = Uranus), an intuitively right understanding of life's aims (Sun/MC = Moon), to seek spiritual contact with others (Mercury/AS = Moon), without avoiding discussions and altercations (Mercury/AS = Uranus), to be successful in discussions and conferences (Mercury/AS = Jupiter). These interpretations also show a positive outlook on life, activity, striving for success, without subordinating one's personal convictions.

The other complex may be interpreted as follows: Emotions and passions are controlled by the intellect and an inner striving toward higher things, (Mars/Neptune) but failures through lack of planning maybe expected; cooperation with others (Mars = Node), the enjoyment of philosophizing with others (Mercury/Saturn = Node), emotional inhibitions (Mercury/Saturn = Neptune), altercations (Mercury/Saturn = Mars).

Although we do get tendencies towards philosophy in this complex, we should not allow ourselves to be led astray by single indications but should investigate whether the individual evidence is confirmed and repeated by other configurations.

One might consider as very negative: MC = Pluto = Sun/Saturn, since this suggests very powerful inhibitions and difficulties in the unfoldment of the personality. Such configurations should not be taken as tragic, but rather as a task imposed to surmount them. If a person is able to accomplish such a task, he may become very great, if however he is unable to, he will not rise above the average.

The individual's task of mastering the natal configuration is the most important aim tendered him by the birth chart, and this therefore constitutes the primary purpose of studying the cosmogram. He who only sees the negative trends in his birth-chart and is therefore becoming afraid of the future had better not occupy himself with this science. If, however, an adviser shows his client only the critical points and scares him (possibly to keep him as a permanent client), he commits a crime, because he contributes to the possible development of the individual's feeling of inferiority and who consequently under certain circumstances may even become unsuitable for work and useless in life.

In our example, the position of Mercury has many more essential factors to reveal, since Mercury = Sun/MC = Venus/Pluto = Node/ AS, indicating the individual's attitude to the outside world and also the tendency to contemplate about himself (Sun/MC), the search for intellectual stimulation through others, versatile interests as well as the readiness to absorb others' thoughts, pleasure in study and research (Node/AS), artistic talent (Venus/Pluto).

Taking these important configurations together, we come to the following conclusions regarding the choice of occupation: providing other circumstances permit (in this case the father was a banker), a scientific vocation is to be preferred, which will allow scope for independent efforts and the representation of own convictions. It is quite possible that occasionally a change of direction or objective will be made and at times unusual difficulties will have to be overcome. Now and again life will bring changes of fortune, but is likely to be successful and to allow the full unfoldment of his own personality.

Karl Jaspers first read law and then studied medicine at various universities and as M. D. became scientific assistant at the Psychiatric Clinic in Heidelberg in 1908. In 1916 he became professor, but in the following years changed over to philosophy and already in 1920 he became extraordinary professor of philosophy and in 1921 professor in ordinary of the University of Heidelberg. The change over to philosophy must have taken place at about 34 years of age (in 1917). If we calculate the solar-arc for this time, we will see in our chart that MCs has reached the complex Mars, Neptune, Node and has just passed the axis Mercury/Saturn. In this complex we not only recognise the interest in philosophy but also MC s = Mercury/Saturn marking the philosopher (CSI 0505). The progressed complex Node, Mars, Neptune commenced to transit the group Jupiter, Moon, Uranus, and when the objective was attained of becoming Extraordinary Professor of philosophy, the midpoint Mercury/Saturn s crossed Neptune. Moon, Uranus, which meant that his study of philosophy (Mercury/Saturn) had already brought recognition (Jupiter).

Naturally, it is likely that shortly before this change of direction there were stagnations in development which led to the decision to transfer from medicine to philosophy. This is characterised by the moving of Pluto s (= Sun/Saturn) over Neptune, Mars, Node, as Pluto and the MC are semi-square and form an axis in the 90°-circle.

For a university scholar who holds and represents his own convictions, it was not easy to assert himself under the Nazi-regime. On the 30th of June, 1937, Karl Jaspers was relieved of his professorship and could only again resume his position in 1945 after the end of the war, when he spoke about the spiritual condition in Germany, a subject he had already dealt with in 1931.

Now was this vocational crisis foreseeable?

When considering a case like this, it should be clear that it is not

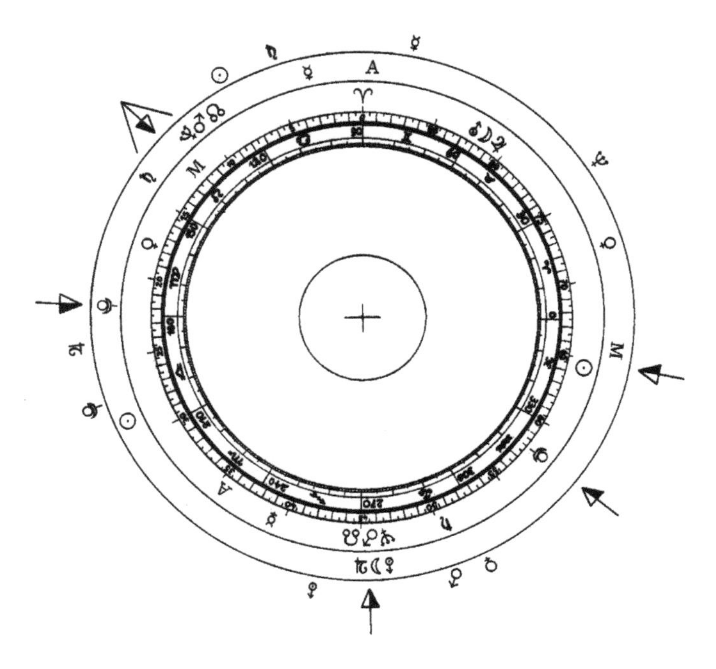

Fig. 41 Prof. Dr. Karl Jaspers

one single day, as here the day of dismissal, that is significant, but that this event is only the outcome of the preceding development, For this reason, one will have to allot a larger field of action to the individual configurations. In Fig. 41 we see that first the complex Jupiter, Moon, Uranus passes over the complex Node, Mars, Neptune. The progressed axis Pluto - MC passes over the solar position, which is in the middle of the two complexes. The natal MC is enclosed by the progressed midpoint, formed by Saturn with the complex Node, Mars, Neptune. Obviously, it is significant that always the same essential configurations of the birth-chart are being re-stimulated. (For further investigations note also the example of Karl Jaspers in *Rapid and Reliable Diagnosis*).

In connection with the existentialism advocated by Jaspers, it is apt to quote here a few sentences by Arthur Hubscher (36) about the philosopher Jaspers. "His attitude has its roots in an original thirst for knowledge (Jupiter = Uranus), his thinking is "activity (Mars) in the domain of his inner self" (Neptune), whether enlightening, arousing, or converting (Moon = Uranus). Again and again it leads to a consciousness of existence, which proves to be something definite, unsurmountable, like illness, struggle, guilt or death like one of those borderline situations, in face of which the real existence, the presence in the world, is severed from the transcendental innermost being (Mars = Neptune)." "He seeks peace by constantly arousing our agitation (Moon = Uranus). All untruth, so he says. springs from the delimitation of religious doctrines. It is no use arguing with religious quarrellers. But all truth is only revealed in the ever new. "now" of the environment, in a steady fathoming of others (Moon = Uranus = Jupiter)." "And when we know that man fails again and again even at his highest and best, this failure has a meaning" (MC = Pluto = Sun/ Saturn).

The cosmogram of the writer Erich Kästner, born February 23, 1899, at 3:45 a.m. in Dresden, has one configuration in common with Jaspers, even so we are dealing with fundamentally different personalities (Fig. 42): MC = Pluto = Sun/Saturn.

Tto this are added a number of midpoints in Kästner's case; since this writer had to work his way up from impoverished conditions, his ascent was very much more difficult. As he was only able to attend school up to age of 13, he afterwards went to a teacher's training college to satisfy his thirst for knowledge and to attain a corresponding position in life. Moreover, he did not want to become a teacher but wanted to continue studying, and did receive a grant. His mother took up a job herself to improve the meagre income of her husband and to be able to help her son.

At 18, under Sun s = Saturn/Neptune, Kästner had to overcome ill health. At the age of 25, he attained his PhD, when Jupiter s had passed the square to the Sun. A life full of variety led to an unusual culmination around the 33rd year. The many difficulties which fate had placed in his cradle through Pluto = MC = Sun/Saturn, only served the urge to survive in spite of the powers that be. Now Jupiter arrived at the opposition to Pluto. The play, "Emil und die

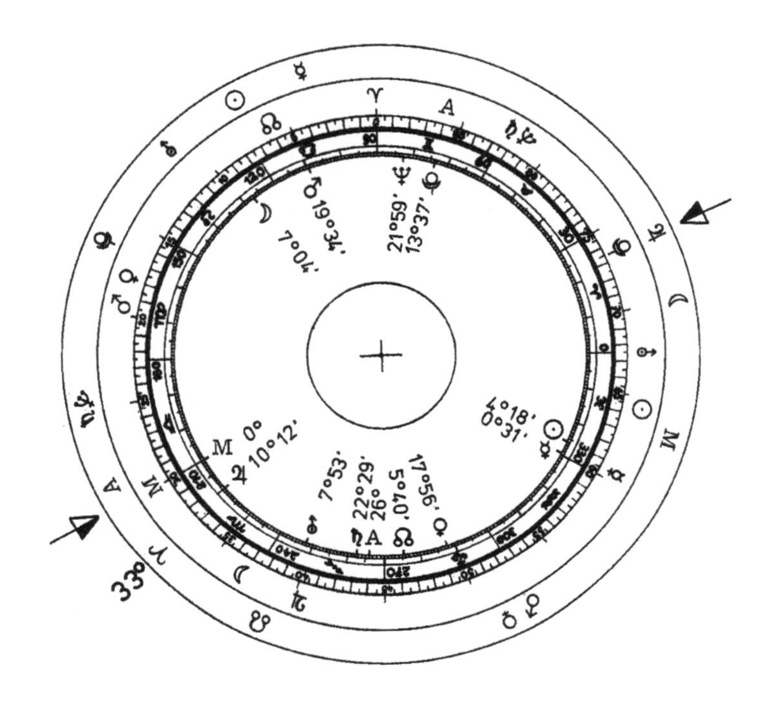

⊖ = M = ☉/♄ = ☉/♆ = ☿/A = ♀/♃ = ♂/♃
☉ = ♂ = ♀ = ☿/♅
☿ = ☽/A = ☽/♄ = ☽/♆ =
♃ = ☿/♂ = ☉/♀
☽ = ♄ = ♆ =
♅ = ☉/⊖ = ♃/☊ = ♂/M = ♀/M

Fig. 42 Erich Kästner

Detective" (Emil and the detectives), brought a huge success and was also made into a film by UFA. Children's novels were published and achieved an enormous circulation, among others, *Das fliegende Klassenzimmer* (the flying classroom). When Hitler came to power, Kästner's books were burnt as undesirable. But in spite of this he was able to win through, and today many of his books are as popular as ever.

This example, too, is intended to show how so-called unfavourable configurations may hamper and delay the development of a person, but cannot stop his advance once the difficulties have been overcome.

Many young people dream of some day becoming a celebrated artist or an actress admired by many. They overlook the fact that "the road to fame is not strewn with flowers" (La Fontaine), but "the road goes over thorns" as a proverb has it. Very often peace of mind or happiness in love have to be sacrificed.

The actor Curt Göetz, born November 17, 1988, was the son of a merchant who died prematurely. His mother opened a clinic which she leased to doctors. His wish to become a doctor could for economic reasons not be realized, and consequently he decided to become an actor, probably without realizing what abilities were latent within him. In a very short time he had become a favorite with the public and was then fairly sure of his success when he opened in his own play. The leading part was taken by himself in this as well as in subsequent plays. These distinguished themselves in that they were smoothly and theatrically written and through lively action and situation comedy enthused the audience. He had the specially good fortune to find a wife who was his best help-mate as well as partner on the stage (Fig. 43).

Looking at the birth-picture we see that the heavenly bodies really have placed the most favorable talents in his cradle, which, based on the positions of the planets in their signs and angular relationships can hardly be envisaged. The most important planetary picture is formed by Jupiter, which, being midway between Sun and Venus, points to a harmonious nature, artistic interests, the power to attract, and popularity. Jupiter also aspects the MC, from which we may deduce: the artist. Additionally, in the 90°-circle we have the Jupiter-MC axis in the middle of the complex Mars, AS, Uranus, and Mercury, with the following significant interpretation: sound judgment, constructive criticism, perseverance, readiness for action, determination, quick wittedness, rich in ideas, clear grasp of every situation, ability to discern relationships, logi-

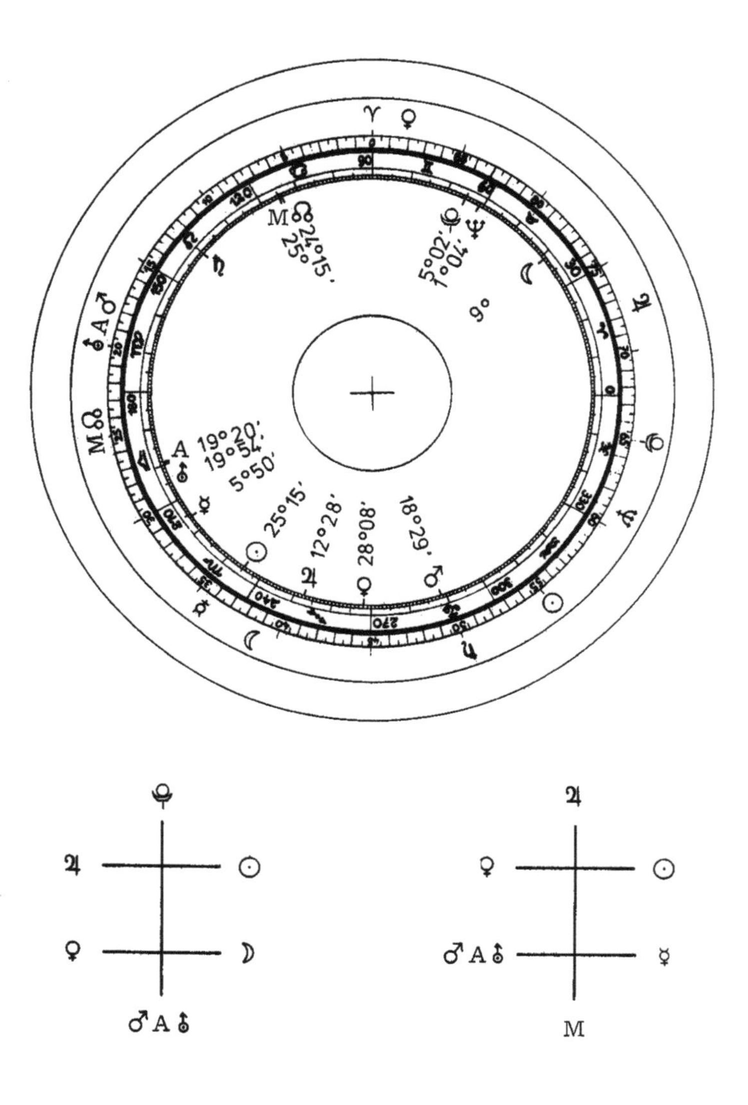

Fig. 43 Curt Göetz

cal deduction, to form and hold one's own opinion, love of conviviality and exchange of thoughts.

Especially significant for success is the Pluto axis. When we place the indicator of the calculating dial on Pluto, the opposite end will point to Uranus, AS, Mars and, additionally, halfway between Sun/Jupiter and Moon/Venus. Accordingly, success (Sun/Jupiter = Pluto) is achieved through an unusually (Pluto) great devotion (Moon/Venus) to a self-imposed task.

For creative artists connections between Sun, Venus, Jupiter, Mercury and Uranus should be extant, of which very many examples may be found. If, indeed, Pluto promises special success such a career may be pursued, but where no corresponding aptitudes are indicated, an artistic career is not advisable. Be warned.

Those who want to occupy themselves with technical subjects, should have especially good contacts between Mars, Uranus and Mercury, to which the usual success configurations have to be added. In this connection, the birth-chart of Ferdinand Porsche, the designer of the Volkswagen, may be of interest. We only know the birthday: September 3, 1875. Porsche was the son of a plumber and was trained in the same trade. At the vocational college his technical ability was recognized. With the support of a far-sighted industrialist he went to Vienna and became an apprentice in an electro-technical factory, and, when only 22, he became head of the test-room. He invented the gear hub engine, and in 1900 at the Paris world exhibition, the electrically propelled Lohner-Porsche-Chaise, constructed by him, caused a sensation. To test his various inventions, he became a racing driver and in 1906 he moved to Daimler-Benz, in Wiener-Neustadt; in 1923 he was transferred to Stuttgart-Unterturkheim to a factory of the same firm, where with his cooperation the Mercedes cars originated. In 1930, he set up his own construction bureaux, and in 1938, he was entrusted with the design and construction of the Volkswagen (Fig. 44).

If we look at the cosmogram, set up for noon. a significant configuration immediately becomes obvious. Mars and Uranus form

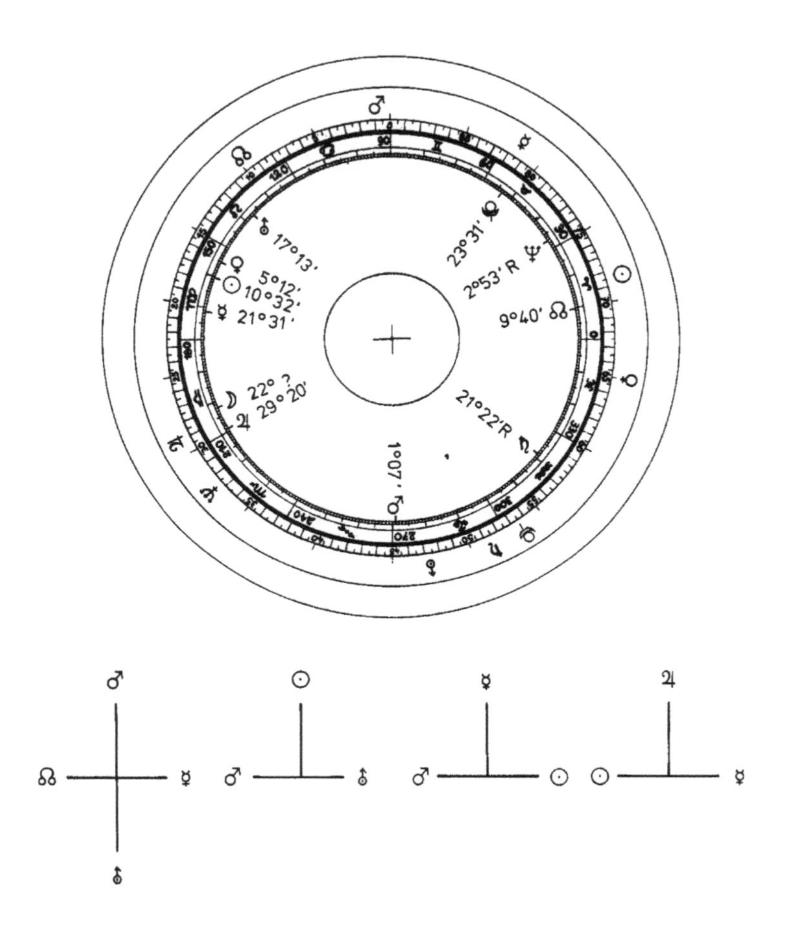

Fig. 44 Ferdinand Porsche

an axis which is cut vertically by the Sun axis. In the 360°-circle, Mars and Uranus are 135° apart, the middle lies at about 25° Libra to which the Sun is in semi-square. Without the dial, these contacts would be hardly noticeable. When Porsche had achieved his first success at 22, as head of the test-room, Sun s reached the semi-square to Uranus and had just passed the square to Mars. When Porsche at the age of 25 caused a sensation at the Paris world exhibition Mars s reached 26° Capricorn in square to Mars/Uranus and in the direction of Jupiter. In 1923, when Porsche transferred to Stuttgart-Unterturkheim, Sun s had almost reached the conjunction to Jupiter. In 1930, when he made himself independent, Mercury s was almost square Uranus.

A close look at the course of a life is necessary to gain some measure of certainty, especially when the hour of birth is unknown. With the above mentioned dates we always find a connection with Mars/Uranus or Sun = Mars/Uranus.

Significant for the successful career is Jupiter = Sun/Mercury. However, there will probably also be contacts with the unknown factors: the MC and AS.

At times it can be difficult to discover the correlations between the occupation and the cosmogram. Very often the job does not correspond to the inherent tendencies, sometimes a sideline may develop into the main occupation and lastly there are various athletes who have achieved greater success in the arena of sport than in their everyday occupation. For this reason, two examples are given here, in which it is hardly possible to discover the occupation from the birth-chart: Georg Thoma, born August 20,1937, at 9 a.m. in Neustadt in the Black Forest, and Oskar Burgbacher, born 10 December, 1925. at 5:45 a.m. in Neikirch near Furtwangen.

Both are postmen by occupation and both have won several ski championships. Georg Thoma was German youth champion three times, in 1959, German cross country champion, won at the 1960 Olympic selections and in the following year was also successful at the Olympics (Fig. 45).

Oskar Burgbacher was German cross country champion several times, second in the postmen's race, first in the road-walk at the championships of the South German states in 1958 at St. Ge-orgen. Burgbacher, however, did not enter for the Winter Olympics (Fig. 46).

It would be useless to look for typical configurations corresponding to skiers and postmen in these two cosmograms. Accord-

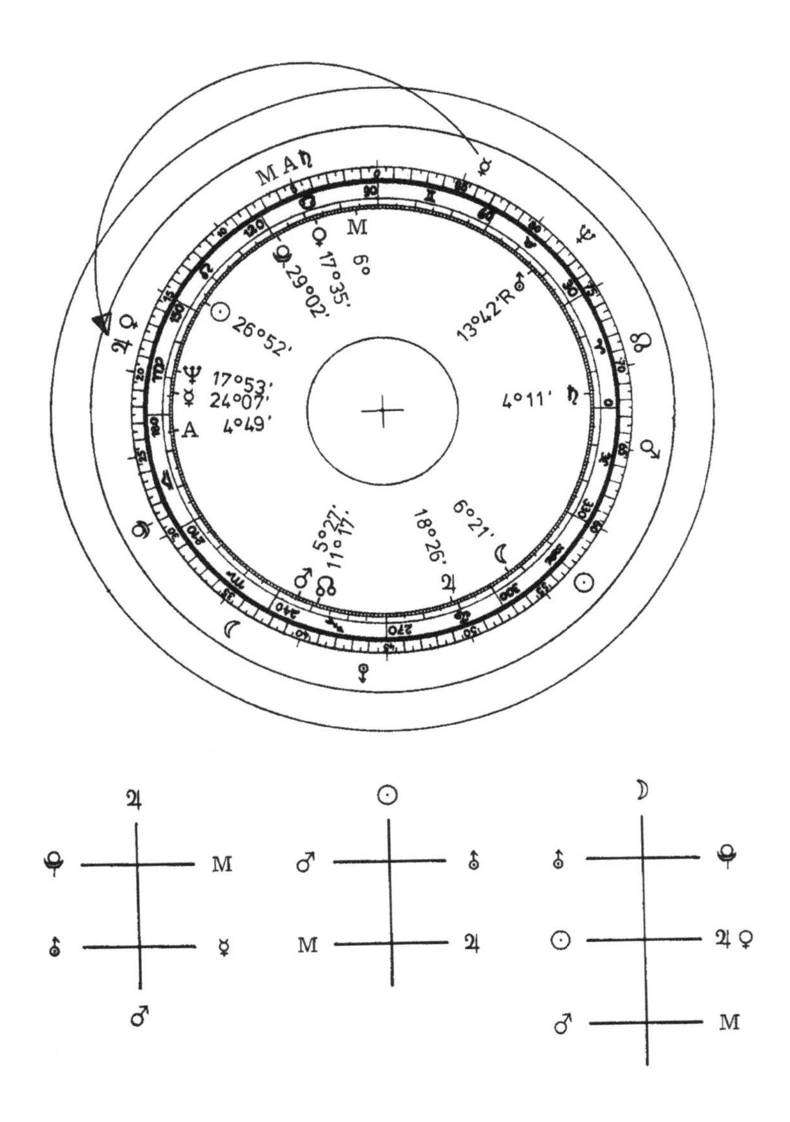

Fig. 45 Georg Thoma

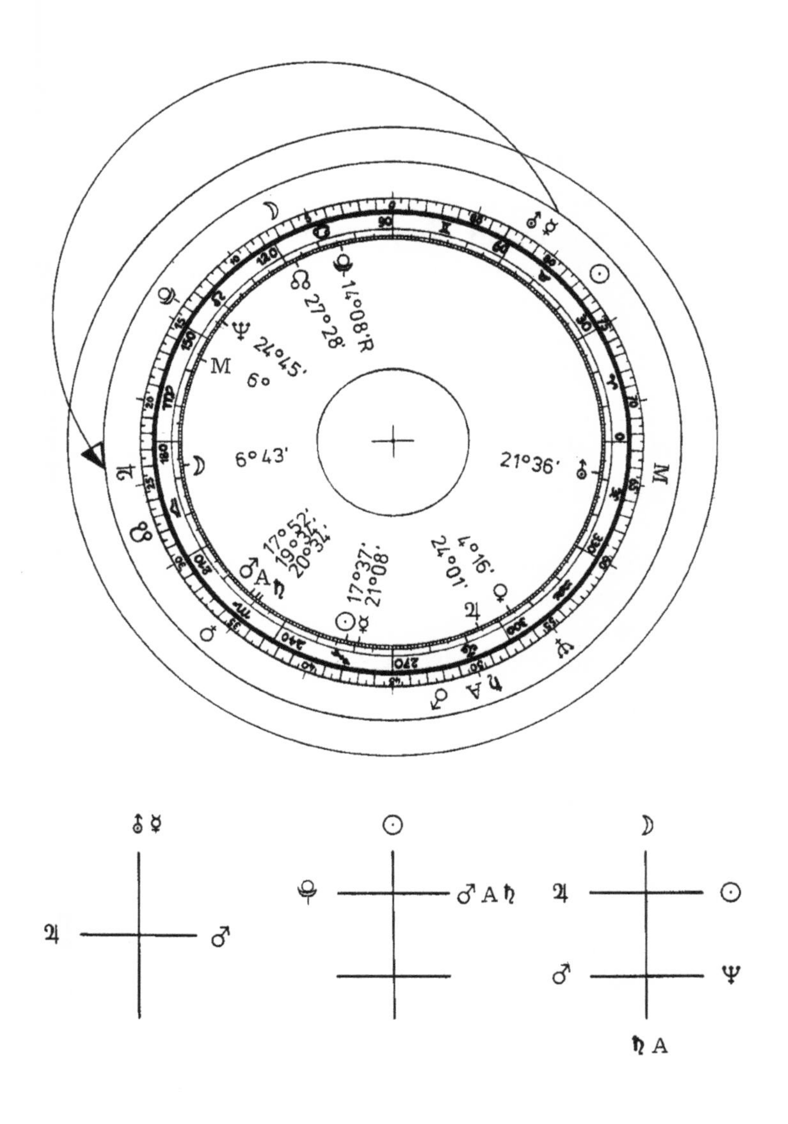

Fig. 46 Oskar Burgbacher

ing to traditional astrology, one would count on a strong emphasis on Mercury (intermediary) and the Moon (people). As corresponding to the sporting activities one could look to Mars (energy), Pluto (unusual achievements), Sun (body), Jupiter (success) in the various angular relationships and midpoints.

In Thoma's birth-chart we find Mercury = Moon/Uranus and in Burgbacher's Mercury square Uranus. These constellations may be correlated with the jobs of the postmen as intermediaries of news. In this case, Mercury is also significator for success in the field of sports, as in both cases championships were won under Mercury s = Jupiter:

Thoma at 24 years: Mercury s - 90 - Jupiter.
Burgbacher at 33 years: Mercury s - 0 - Jupiter.

We also find similar configurations in both cases:

Thoma	*Burgbacher*
Moon = Sun/Jupiter	Moon = Sun/Jupiter
Uranus = Mars/Jupiter	Uranus = Mercury = Mars/Jupiter
Sun = Mars/Uranus	Sun = Mars/Pluto
Jupiter = Mercury/Uranus = Mars	Mercury = Uranus = Mars/Jupiter

In both cases there is connection between Saturn and AS. With Burgbacher we may suspect a lack of contact-ability, as in spite of his successes at home, he has not taken part in any of the world-championships. Thoma also appears to have, a reserved nature. These qualities, however, are not to be associated with the activity.

This example is also intended to show how investigations should be done to determine the matching configurations of people following the same occupations. Unfortunately, up to now it has not been possible to form work-teams to undertake such investigations on a larger scale in order to achieve a surer foundation for this work.

Although in this book the occupational problem has been given much space, it has in no way been exhausted. However, it may be that the ideas offered here will stimulate your own private investigation.

Winning Configurations

The question is repeatedly asked as to whether it is possible with the aid of the cosmogram to calculate when one could win in the foot-ball pool, raffle, or lottery, etc. If it were as easy as that, then all those occupying themselves with this science would have won many times over and be very rich, in any case, it is not as simple as those "systems" to be found in newspaper advertisements would have one believe. I myself have tried it out and even under the most favorable configurations I have not won anything. Once I tried an experiment with the help of a weekly paper. Of 30,000 readers, during the course of several months, three notified me who had won a worthwhile sum. These were people in whose cosmograms gains through speculation had been indicated. (Neptune-Jupiter combinations). The following example is only intended to show what cosmic correlations are to be found when someone does indeed win. It will be seen that this is not a case of "lucky stars" being instantly obvious. A reader of the *Kosmische Beobachter* wrote to us:

"On 1 November, 1957, my son won a prize of 1, 000 DM, a very nice sum for a journeyman painter." The son was born September 8, 1922, at 5.45 a.m. in Kamen (Fig. 47).

Calculating the solar-arc for the year concerned, we see that a lucky chance is quite possible through:

Sun s conjunction Jupiter r
19°12' Libra 19°46' Libra

If we now place the transiting planets in the outer 90°-circle, it is immediately apparent that transiting Jupiter moves towards Ju-

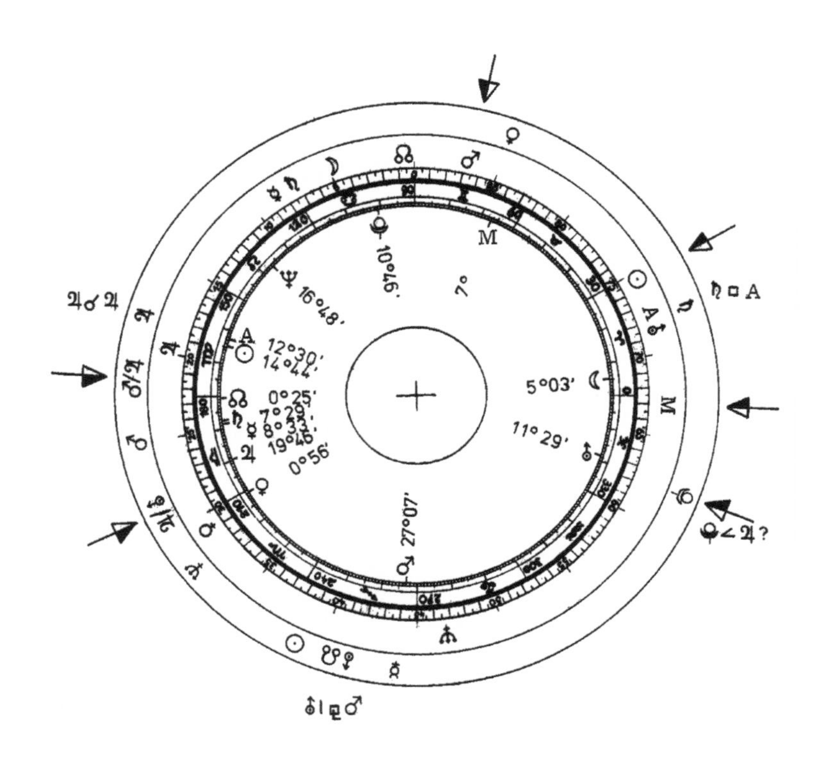

☉ s ☌ ♃ r
19°12 ♎ 19°46 ♎

♅ l ♇ ♂ r = ♃/M r
♂/♃ l = M r
♃ l = ⊖ l = ♃ r
17°54 1°56 19°46
(16°56)
♃/♅ l = ☉ r
<u>14°43</u> <u>14°44</u>

Fig. 47 A Win of DM 1000

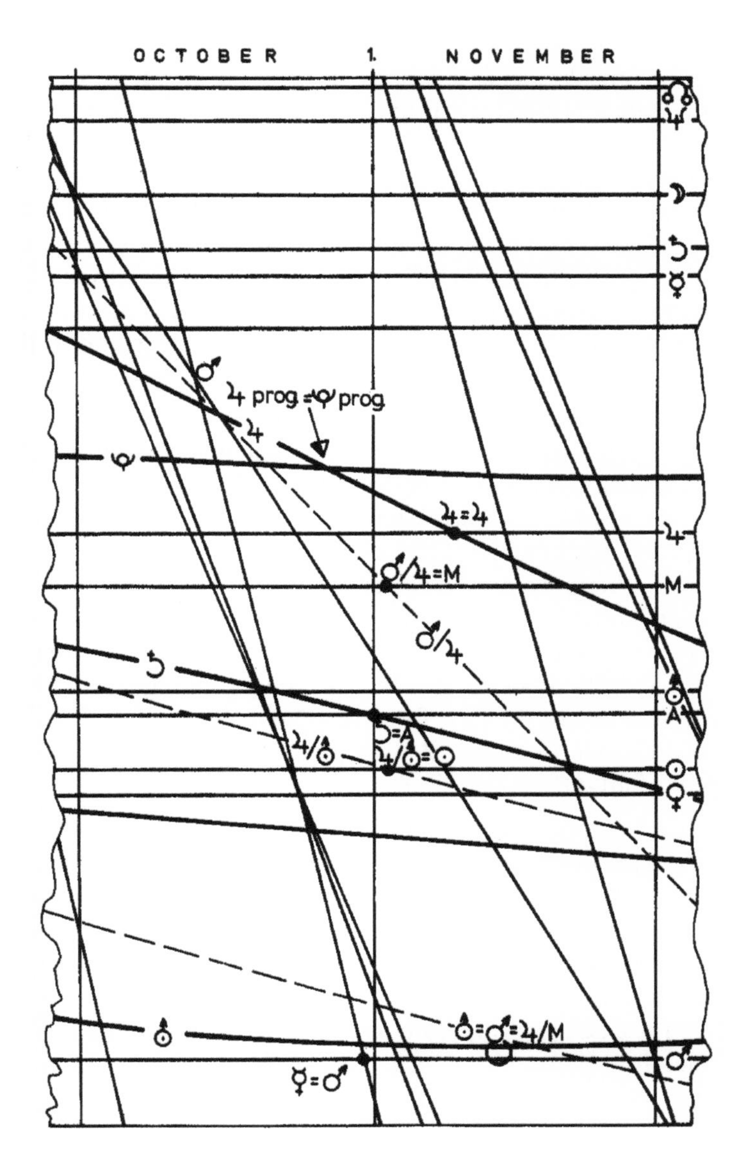

Fig. 48 A Win of DM 1000

piter r and is almost exactly opposite Pluto t. It is obvious, that only some days later did the young man get the most pleasure from the money, when he was able to use it to purchase something special. It is a little more difficult to see that midpoint Mars t/ Jupiter t coincide with MC on the other side. Lastly we spot below: transiting Uranus opposition Mars in the axis Jupiter/MC (personal success, personal happiness). Absolutely exact to the minute, Jupiter/Uranus is in the Sun axis with the indication of sudden happiness. On the other hand, Saturn = AS does not seem to be the aspect to signify gain; it is not known whether any difficulties arose subsequently.

This example shows that not only the directions and transits are significant, the midpoints have to be included. Additionally, Fig. 48 depicts the cosmogram in the 45°-midpoint ephemeris diagram. If one follows the line of Jupiter, one will see that Jupiter in connection with Pluto is in an especially favourable "cosmic condition", therefore one may deduce that shortly before this transit over Jupiter and MC of the birth-chart, a largish success or advantage may be predicted. One will note that Uranus is shortly due to turn retrograde so that in this way a longer lasting and more powerful transit with Mars is formed, although this aspect does not become exact. However, this does confirm that in cases like this an orb of up to 1° is permissible.

The natal configurations on the graphic ephemeris only indicate when the transits are due. However, it is necessary in each case, using the dial, to take a closer look at the cosmic conditions of the natal planets and the transiting planets as well in order to draw the corresponding conclusions. Particularly the Uranus-Mars-configuration would otherwise warrant a completely different interpretation if natal Mars were not on Jupiter/MC. For a prediction, it is therefore advisable to use both methods (the 90°-dial and the graphic ephemeris) simultaneously.

Man in the Universe Geocentric and Heliocentric Observations

The individual is always, to a certain degree, linked to universal happenings and conditions. It may be that his mood is influenced by the weather, that he is dependent on the climate in which he lives, that an event in the air or on earth disrupts his thoughts, or that he will be influenced by the people in his personal or occupational environment. For this reason, as many varied observations as possible should be made in order to discern the many threads intertwining the cosmos, earth and humanity. These threads are like many invisible rays, but one senses their presence and they may partly even be calculated in advance.

These facts often go beyond the limit of imagination, so that they have to be illustrated by primitive examples.

If we place a chicken egg upon the earth, we can imagine that the egg and the earth are in a similar relationship as the earth and the solar system. In the egg is life, it may be hatched and the chick become a hen. Manifold are the influences which may effect the egg, against which the life inside is unable to defend itself. The egg may be endangered by a knock, heat or cold, a bird may peck at it, it may be eaten up by an animal or used by a human for cooking. Just as the egg is vulnerable to numerous influences, the earth is also subject to the manifold influences of the cosmic manifestations with no possibility of resistance. Man on earth can only adapt himself to the various influences or, alternatively, use them for his own ends through his individual capacities.

As long as man considered the earth as a world apart, he was only able to regard the total happenings from the viewpoint of the earth, what he could see with his own eyes. He was restricted to "earthly" seeing and thinking. However, his view widened into limitlessness, when it was recognized that the earth is not the universe but a part of the solar system in a universe containing many more fixed star systems.

Each heavenly body should not to be regarded as an inert body, but as a factor of activity which not only changes through its movements in relationship to other heavenly bodies but also by collaboration with other heavenly bodies. Observations have repeatedly shown, that certain angular relationships play apart, but which produce a completely different picture, depending on whether the earth or the sun is chosen as the angular point, whether the heavenly bodies in their angular configurations are heliocentrically or geocentric ally observed. This is best shown with the graphic ephemeris. (Fig. 49)

In the heliocentric presentation at the top, planetary courses run straight (minimal deviations are hardly discernible with the naked eye); in the geocentric chart, the planets apparently move in more or less strong curves. These curves result from the apparent progressive and retrograde motion of the heavenly bodies, as they are given in the yearly ephemeris. Only the lines of the Sun and earth are identical, because when transferred to the degree-circle these are always opposed to each other. (We are using this ☉ as the symbol for the Sun, because the reversed Venus symbol for earth might easily cause confusion.)

In order to facilitate the identification of the various representations, we are marking the geocentric data with g and the heliocentric ones with h.

The charts show only sections of the degrees 30-45 in the 45°-degree system as has previously been explained. Observe mainly the lines of Saturn and Neptune. Geocentric ally they touch

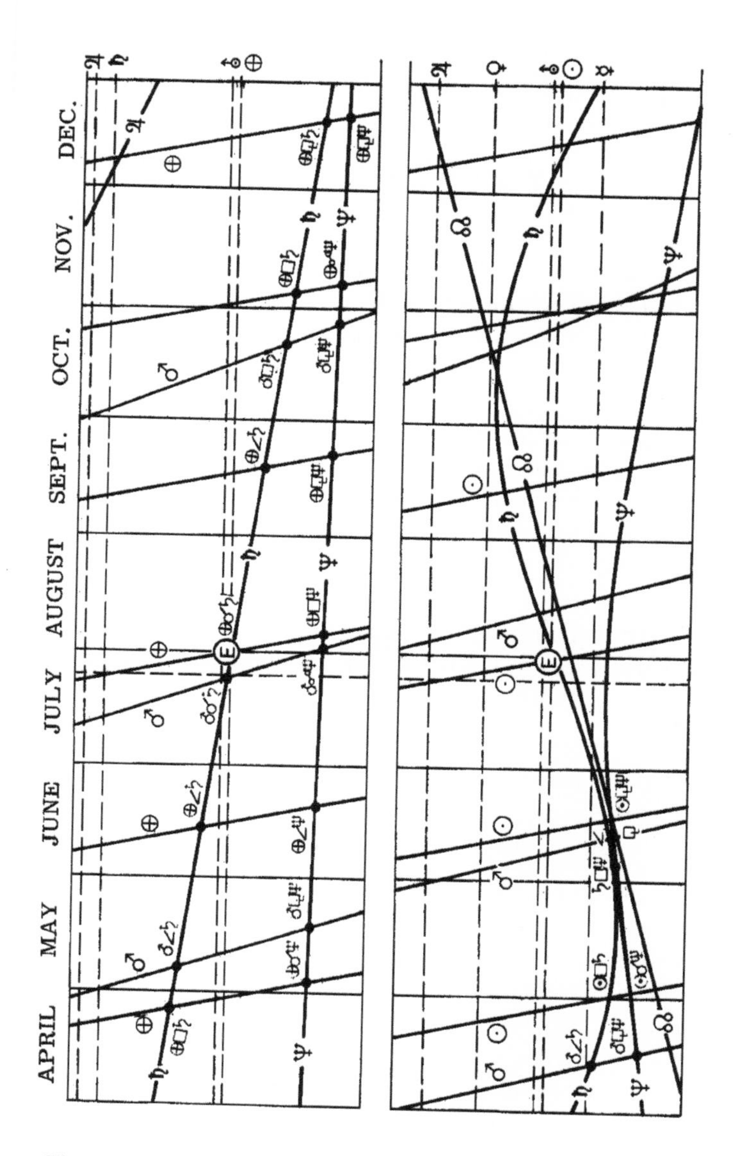

Fig. 49 Extracts from the heliocentric and geocentric graphic 45°-ephemeris for 1962.

each other (only apparently of course) in June 1962, and heliocentrically for the first time in January 1963, when the lines also cross, geocentrically, a second time.

Readers of the *Kosmische Beobachter* may recall that the May 1962 issue carried a similar illustration as a cover picture with the title *World Illness - World Crisis*. At that time the damp and cold weather just did not seem to come to an end; right into the summer one had to keep turning on the heating. In consequence of the bad weather the number of cases of sickness increased to such an extent that all hospitals were overcrowded (referring to Germany particularly). In Berlin, 20,000 people contracted dysentery. Repeatedly cases of smallpox occurred. On the New York stock exchange an economic world crisis became plainly evident on May the 28th, and as a consequence, European exchange values collapsed on May the 29th. The USA lost milliards. At that time. on May 29th, Saturn square Neptune g was due exactly to the minute. In this critical period, the mass exodus of Europeans from Algeria also took place. In the German Federal Republic a decisive political crisis was in the offing on account of Chancellor Adenauer's waning authority, even within his own party.

It seems odd that corresponding heliocentric configurations were not due at this time. But when in January 1963, Saturn square Neptune became exact, "a black day for Europe" resulted through the failure of the economic conference in Brussels.

The *Kosmische Beobachter* repeatedly pointed out that the individual configurations would especially be felt by those people whose radical positions could be brought into connection with the stellar combinations. In order to capture a portion of the overall picture, the systematic procedure for prognostication will be shown. For the investigation we will use the magnetic dial; for the purposes of a clear explanation, however, we shall have to keep within certain limits.

In Fig.50, the diurnal positions have been entered heliocentrically and geocentrically. The heliocentric positions are within the

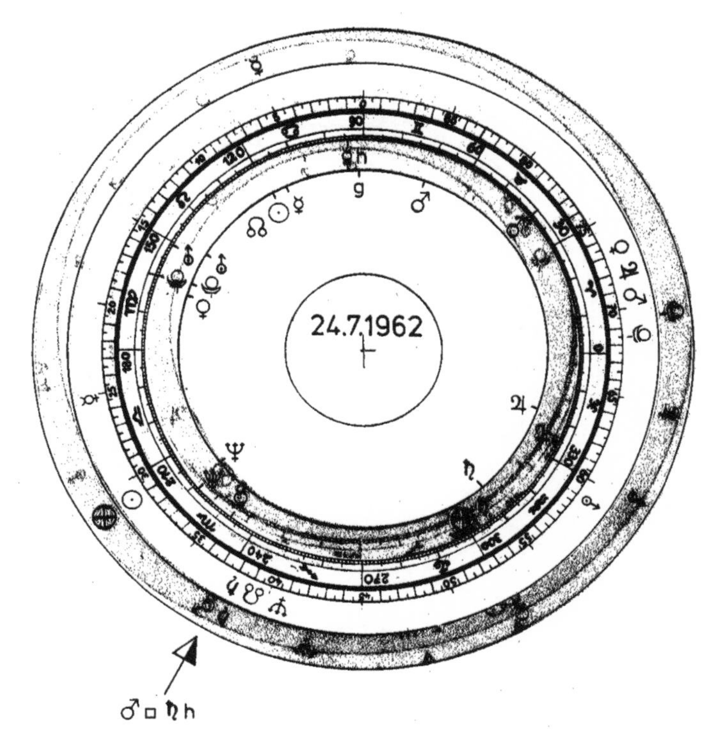

Fig. 50

yellow circles, inside in the 360° system, and outside in the 90°-circle: the date chosen is July 24, 1962.

Firstly, we can clearly see the differences in the positions of the stellar bodies. Sun and earth always have to be in opposition. Mercury h is in the beginning and Mercury g at the end of the sign Cancer. Venus h moves in Scorpio, Venus g in the sign Virgo, Mars h is in Taurus, Mars g in Gemini. With the slow movers the differences are significantly smaller. In the outer 90°-circle the angular relationships are immediately obvious.

Fig. 51 shows the configurations a few days later, on 1 August, 1962. Here we recognize at once the connection of the Sun or earth

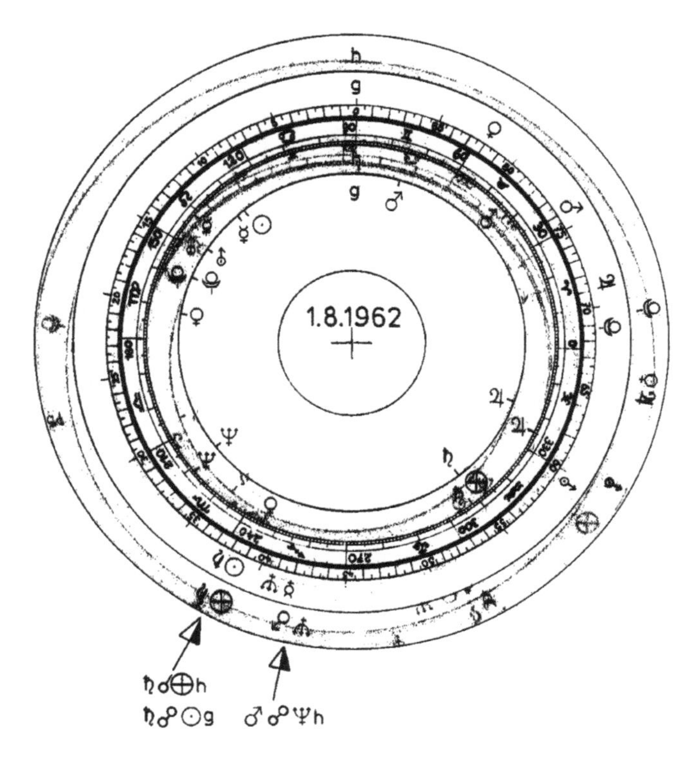

Fig. 51

respectively with Saturn and Mars h with Neptune h.

Based on these configurations the following predictions were made in the July issue of the *Kosmische Beobachter*: A very critical time may be expected the 19th-23rd of July through Mars square Pluto g on the 21st and Mars square Saturn h on the 23rd. Force majeure, natural catastrophes and transportation disasters can be anticipated. In the days around the 26th, square Jupiter may correspond to special decisions or the solving of problems. Since between the middle of July and the beginning of August transiting Uranus comes into contact with Dr. Adenauer's and De Gaulle's solar positions, it may be possible that at this time changes affecting France and Germany may come about. At the end of the month, Sun and Mercury are in opposition to Saturn, joined by Mars square Neptune h. Between the 28th and the 31st of July, there is a danger of the weather worsening, very unfriendly and cold days may be expected and in a few districts danger from floodwater.

These predictions have in the main been confirmed, a priore observing that in many cases the constellations are activated before they are exact. Under Mars square Saturn h on the 23rd, a number of disasters occurred: on 22nd July, damage running to millions is caused in Zurich through a gigantic fire, a railway accident in India results in 39 dead and 44 injured, the derailment of a holiday express in France, 47 dead, an air-crash in California, 3 dead on the 23rd, an air-crash in Honolulu has 27 killed, and many other small traffic accidents. Simultaneously, the situation in Peru came to a head through a government coup, in Algeria Ben Bella was successful in the struggle and founded a political bureau for power. Dr. Adenauer's position became disturbed by a new "war of nerves" in Berlin, as well as through the affairs of Strauss, Fränkel, Globke and others, and he was urged to clear up matters. De Gaulle was kept in a state of disquiet-ment by the happenings in Algeria.

As had been predicted through Sun opposition Saturn and earth conjunct Saturn, seasonly severe cold weather set in, during the last days of the month.

When Mars was square Neptune h on the 31st, terrible weather conditions did not fail to cause havoc. In Bavaria, 90% of the harvest was destroyed, in the Philippines 60 people died in floods. We may recall that the flood catastrophe in Hamburg happened shortly before Mars square Neptune g. Further unusual catastrophes occurred during those days: three severe earthquakes in Columbia, 200 workers were buried underneath a textile factory, a factory-hall collapsed in Schwerte, several air-crashes occurred.

Now it must be specially pointed out that we are dealing here-

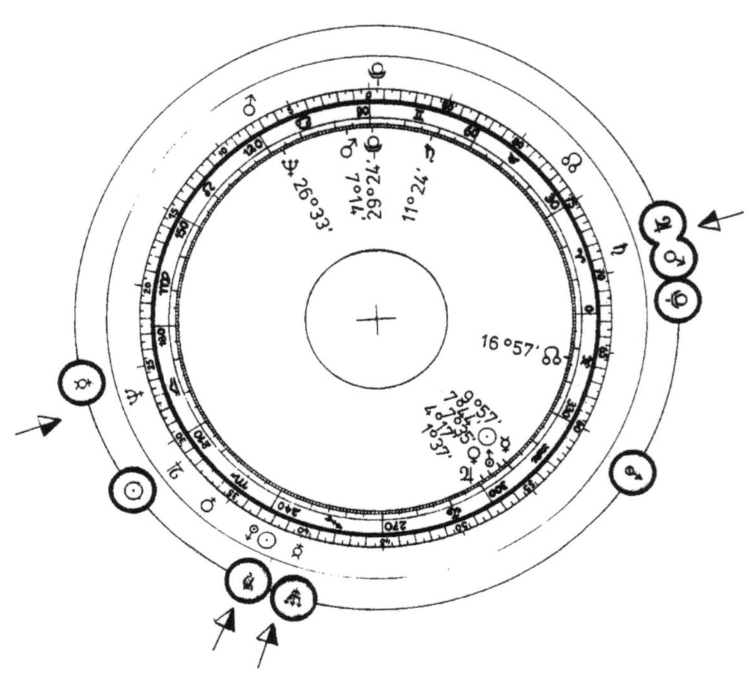

Fig. 52 The little circles (Figs. 52 and 53) represent the magnets and mark the positions of the transiting planets. The outer circle of the magnetic 90°-dial has a diameter of 20 cm allowing ample room for entering the geocentric and heliocentric positions. Here we are restricted by the size of the book, making a clear reproduction of the combined picture impossible. For this reason, the heliocentric and the geocentric pictures have been printed separately.

with heliocentric configurations, which however also confirm the experiences gained from geocentric data. From this and many other cases the necessity is obvious of observing the geocentric and heliocentric planetary movements simultaneously, which with the aid of the magnetic dial is easily done.

The experiences as provided by world affairs are also confirmed in private life. As an example, let us take the case Schlicker. On the 24th July, it was announced that the Schlicker ship-yard

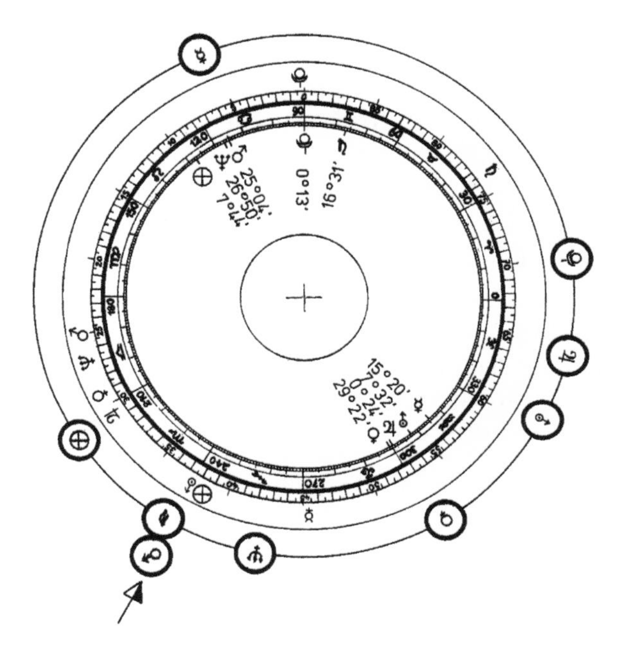

Fig. 53

was in difficulties. The following day another ship-yard stated that it could not meet its obligations. In Figs. 52 and 53 the birth-chart of the yard owner is depicted geocentrically and heliocentrically. As the exact birth time is not known we have to be satisfied with the configurations of that day. The transiting planets are marked in yellow.

It should be noted specially, that after the Second World War Willy Schlicker only had a starting capital of 3,600 DM and an old Opel-Blitz car. In a very short time he developed his enterprises so successfully that quite recently his net profit was 4,000 DM per hour.

Now with one stroke the Schlicker shipyard collapsed. The ships already under construction, worth many millions in DM, had to be transferred to other shipyards.

In the graphic ephemeris we have already seen from the dotted horizontal position lines that. in Fig. 49 in the heliocentric chart, the transiting planets Mars and Saturn pass over the Earth and Uranus at the end of July. In the geocentric chart we observe that a few days later Saturn will pass over Sun and Uranus, while Saturn and Neptune have been close to Mercury for some time which means that the world-crisis configuration referred to earlier involved Mercury in this personal cosmogram.

One will have to admit that the seriousness of the crisis corresponds to heliocentric Mars with Saturn, while the geocentric configurations had already occurred. Although we do not have the birth time to compute the exact positions, we will nevertheless make a comparison in degrees and minutes:

Geocentrically due:
Neptune t 10°43' Scorpio = Mercury r 9°57' Aquarius
Saturn t 8°36' Aquarius = Uranus r 7°35' Aquarius
Saturn t 8°36' Aquarius = Sun r 7°44' Aquarius
Jupiter t 11°54' Pisces = Saturn r 11°24' Gemini
Mars t 10°41' Gemini = Saturn r 11°24' Gemini
Sun t 1°06'Leo = Jupiter r 1°37' Aquarius
Mercury t 25°10' Cancer = Neptune r 26°33' Cancer
Sun t 1°06' Leo = Jupiter r 1°37' Aquarius
Heliocentrically due:
Saturn t 7o50' Aquarius = Uranus r 7o32' Aquarius
Saturn t 7o50' Aquarius = Earth r 7o44' Leo
Mars t 7o59' Taurus = Uranus r 7o32' Aquarius
Mars t 7o59' Taurus = Earth r 7o44' Leo
Earth 1o06' Aquarius = Jupiter r 0o24' Aquarius
Earth 1o06' Aquarius = Saturn r 16o31' Gemini

Investigating the individual constellations including their midpoint positions we get the following definitions:

Geocentrically:

Jupiter t = Mars t = Saturn r = Neptune r: fluctuating success, annoyance, trouble, all efforts of will meet with resistance, test of strength, disagreements, separations, unfortunate speculations, losses, failures caused through lack of planning or lack of energy, weakness.

Neptune t = Mercury = Mars/Saturn r: self deception, lack of clarity, failures, hopelessness, insufficient power to tackle resistance or obstacles, weakening power, weariness.

Saturn t = Sun r = Uranus r = Pluto/Node: enforced modesty and simplicity, suppression by others, separations, to fight against oppression, to be troubled by one's environment, intervention in fate, enforced severing of connections.

Sun t = Jupiter r = Node r = Sun/Neptune = Uranus/Neptune: optimism, sensitivity, shared suffering (daily influences are operative here, while the other configurations are of longer duration).

Heliocentrically:

Saturn t = Mars t = Uranus r= Earth r = Saturn/Pluto = Mercury/Jupiter: enforced release of tensions, challenge to decisive battle, intervention in fate, delays in formulating decisions, uncertainty during negotiations, discussions.

Earth t = Jupiter r = Mars/Uranus r = Earth/Mars r = Saturn: on this day there is still hope for a happy turn of events through a correct grasp and understanding of the situation and taking corresponding steps.

One will remember that first of all everything was tried to save the enterprise, but later, all hope was given up.

The value of this method lies in the fact that man is placed within the whole, which additionally influences but in no way determines his individual fate. Man cannot avoid the configurations that are due, but he can prepare plan his actions accordingly; dangers may not be wholly avoided but they can be minimized.

Recently, I have become accustomed, with the aid of the magnetic dial, to making continuous observations of the geocentric and heliocentric positions, and which has proved to be of success in prognostication.

Progressed Aspects

The secondary directions, or progressions, should be ranged next to the solar-arc directions as yet one other system which has proved itself time and again. While the key to the solar-arc directions is:

1 day's movement of the Sun (about 1 degree) = 1 year of life, the rule for the progressions is:

1 day after birth = 1 year of life.

When working with solar-arc directions the positions of all the factors are moved forward by equal distances of about one degree for each year of life, hence the suitability of the dial for this method. On the other hand, when using progressions the individual daily movements of the stellar bodies have to be specially calculated for each year under consideration. A simple way is to add the number of days corresponding to the years of life to the birth day and to check if on any day important aspects to the birth configurations are formed. The positions of the Sun s and Sun p (p = progressive) are always identical. With the progressions the positions of those bodies are significant which are close together in the birth-chart and are moving toward or away from each other, that is, are direct or retrograde. This fact may be of decisive importance.

Let us look at the chart of Hanns Porst, which has been investigated in detail in *Rapid and Reliable Analysis* (37). In this case, Saturn is retrograde 18°52' Scorpio square Sun at 20°40' Aquarius. As Saturn moves in retrogression, Saturn p square Sun never becomes exact. Consequently, this inhibition aspect cannot have its corresponding effect. On the other hand, it Saturn p, during the course of life, becomes exact we may in cases expect greater difficulties concerning health or occupation, but which despite their severity may also bring rich experiences and understanding.

When aspects of Uranus and Jupiter become exact by progression there is often a complete change in life or a special success.

The dial is used to investigate and evaluate the individual positions and their midpoints. President John Kennedy had Uranus at 23°43' Aquarius. On the same day, Uranus turned retrograde and moved extraordinarily slowly. Jupiter was at 23°04' Taurus, these planets were therefore 90°39' apart. Jupiter had passed the square to Uranus only three days later, however, the retrograding Uranus needed 41 days, that is 41 years, to make the aspect exact, corresponding to 1958. In 1956, Kennedy was already a presidential candidate; he was elected in 1960, when Uranus had passed the square to Jupiter by three minutes.

If we adjust the indicator of the calculating dial to Jupiter, it will be on the midpoint Pluto/Node with the interpretation as given in the CSI:

"The desire to obtain position and power by force through the help of others."

Pluto/Node is a significator for mass meetings and associations, concerns. We only have to think of the many mass meetings Kennedy addressed in order to win the necessary votes for the presidential office.

Exemplary in a negative sense is the cosmogram of Adolf Hitler. Here, Mars is at 16°23' Taurus and Saturn at 13°27' Leo. The planets are only about three degrees apart. Saturn p makes the square exact 54 days = years later, that is, in 1943. At this time, his luck completely deserted him, the disaster of Stalingrad decided the war to his disadvantage, in 1944 an attempt was made on his life, and on 30 April, 1945, he committed suicide. In the 90°-circle Mars is on Sun/Pluto, the midpoint of craving for rulership and the desire for power. Mars helped him to attain power, but to some extent the progressive Saturn took it from him and also took his life.

Concluding Remarks

Even in consideration of the many examples from various spheres of life shown here, the possible applications of cosmobiology in general and the 90°-dial in particular are in no way exhausted.

However, I do hope to have given a broad basis to all friends of cosmobiology upon which further progress may be founded. If various questions still remain open, I shall be grateful for all suggestions which perhaps may be dealt with in a second volume.

When drafting the manuscript I had numerous valuable suggestions from Mr. Hans Hausmann and from my son Dr. Baldur R. Ebertin, to whom I would like to extend my special thanks. With the handing over of this book to those interested I would also like to thank all those who have participated in furthering and widening my research and, through new ideas and investigations, also in expanding the whole field of cosmobiology. Despite the untiring effort of a small research group, we are really only at the beginning of a new true cosmobiology, but we may be certain of the fact that the chosen path will lead to the creation of a new science.

Explanation of Terms Used in this Book

Angles, see aspects.

AS = A = Ascendant: this is the point where the ecliptic cuts the eastern horizon. In the figures the letter A is used, in the text AS has been preferred in order to avoid mistakes.

Aspect really means "view-point" and denotes the angle at which the individual factors "look at" each other, or their angular relationship.

Contact-cosmograms are charts consisting of concentrically connected 90°-circles, which enable the entering of several cosmograms simultaneously in order to be able to determine favourable or unfavourable contacts and also to establish possible favourable or critical periods (for instance in marriage, working partnerships etc.).

Correspondence may be understood as some sort of up to now unexplained connection between the configurations of the heavenly bodies and events occurring on earth. The word correspondence is used especially where one cannot speak of a planetary influence.

Cosmobiology, see the explanation in the Introduction.

CSI is the abbreviation generally used for *Combination of Stellar Influences*.

Degree Directions rest on the theory that the movement or progressions of the individual factors by one degree correspond to one year of life.

Directions may be called movements within the cosmogram; from this movement of two (or more factors) the time of a possible realization of an event maybe determined. The directions do not correspond to actual movements in the heavens as do transits.

Factor refers to a co-deciding reason or one-of-several co-deciding links. In this sense "factors" comprise all "co-affecting" elements, by which Sun, Moon, Moon's Node, AS, MC, and so on, are meant.

Fixed Stars are apparently stationary stars, whose movement is so slight that it cannot be detected with the naked eye, but it can be computed.

Heavenly Bodies is the collective description of the Sun, Moon and the Planets. When in astrology, Sun and Moon are referred to as planets, this is obviously incorrect. The Sun is not a planet but a fixed star, neither is the Moon a planet but a satellite of the earth.

K1 and K2 are abbreviations used for the two charts combining the 360°-circle with the 90°-circle. K1 may be used as pocket-size edition for charts the size of the illustrations in this book. K2 is a larger work chart intended for use with the dial.

m = Abbreviation for Male, w = Abbreviation for Female or Woman (the translator has adhered to the German abbreviation for mannlich = m, and weiblich = w in order to comply with the symbols used in the illustrations).

Malefics is a term that was used to describe planets whose action was said to be detrimental (Mars, Saturn) to differentiate them from the benefics that, according to "the old belief in the stars," were favourably disposed towards humanity. For us these fatalistic conceptions are now defunct. However, it is difficult to find an appropriate substitute. It would be better to speak of negative and positive, although we have to realize that every "nature" contains positive and negative elements in varying proportions.

MC = M = Medium Coeli refers to the point of culmination or meridian, which at the moment of birth, or of an event, is at a vertical angle to the (birth) place. Within the cosmogram, the letter M is to be preferred, but in the text we have used MC (similar as with A = AS) in order to avoid mix-ups.

Mid-points are angular relationships, in which one factor forming an axis is equidistant to two other factors, one on each side, - measured on the degree-circle. Mathematically, the middle factor is in the halfsum of the positions of the other two factors calculated from 0° Aries.

Naibod Arc is the mean daily movement of the Sun, which is about 57° to 1°01'.

Nature of the Heavenly Bodies. Without reference to the various deities whose names they bear, experience has shown that each planet has different qualities or that they reveal themselves in different ways. Even popular language for instance denotes Mars as fiery, Saturn as cold, Venus as lovely. Under the nature of the heavenly bodies we understand their qualities as these have been determined by experience.

Orb. The angular relationships of the planets are not only valid when exact to the minute, a certain deviation or "orb" on either side is allowed. With the aspects 3°, 4° and 5°, with midpoints 1½° are allowed. In traditional astrology orbs of up to 15° are acceptable but this is untenable.

p = Progressive. The progression of the heavenly bodies (as directions) is calculated according to the measure of 1 day after birth corresponding to one year of actual life. Therefore, these types of directions are called progressive and the abbreviation used is p. (The author differentiates between progressed aspects p and solar-arc directions s. The abbreviation for the solar-arc directions is s for solar-arc.)

r = Radix = Root. This refers to the birth cosmogram, to distinguish it from other planetary configurations (p, s, t).

Release. Once certain configurations, structures, etc. have been found in the cosmogram. one will wish to know the time when the tendencies shown in the birth configuration are likely to mature, that is when they will be released (or manifested or resolved).

s instead of the abbreviation "v" used hitherto, standing for "vorgeschoben" (= advanced), it is preferable to use "s" to indicate advanced factors based on solar-arc.

Solar Arc is that arc of the zodiac which the sun traverses in a given time. The daily advance of the Sun corresponds to one year of life. The other factors of the birth-chart are advanced by this same arc.

Structure Picture. This could be called composite picture, containing of the various structural elements emerging from the "cosmic condition" of the individual factors.

Symbols are the emblems denoting the heavenly bodies; for instance a circle with a dot in the centre represents the Sun, the crescent represents the Moon etc. Today these symbols are no longer to be considered as having symbolic meaning, because the planetary signs have been derived from Greek letters.

t = Transiting. This is the abbreviation for a moving planet (according to the movement in the daily ephemeris) contrary to the fixed positions of the heavenly bodies at the moment of birth. The term transits is also used for the passage of the t-planets over the birth positions and their angular points.

v = "vorgeschoben," see "s".

References

Boll-Betzold, Sternglaube und Sterndeutung, Leipzig, 1950.

Robert Henseling, Umstrittenes Weltbild, Leipzig, 1940.

H.A. Strauss, editor of the “Jahrbuch fur kosmobiologische Forschung,” Augsburg, 1928. Reinhold Ebertin, author of the report, “Kongress astrologischer Pioniere,” Erfurt, 1932. Reinhold Ebertin, editor of the “Jahrbuch fur kosmobiologische Forschung” since 1938.

Prof. R. Tomaschek, “Great Earthquakes and the Astronomical Positions of Uranus,” *Nature* (London) 184, pp. 177-8 (1959), 186, pp. 337- 8 (1960).

Theodor Landscheidt, Fixsterne, Aspekte und galaktische Strukturen, Aalen, 1965. Cosmopsychogramm: see Die kosmischen Grundlagen unseres Lebens, Reinhold und Baldur Ebertin, Aalen, 1955, in which for the first time the basic foundations are clearly expounded. Theodor Landscheidt, Direktionen - Zahlen - Strukturen, Aalen, 1961.

Reinhold Ebertin, Transite, Gorlitz, 1927, Aalen 1948/52; English edition, *Transits*, Aalen, 1971. Reinhold Ebertin, Sternenbahnen - Weltgeschehen - Menschenwege, Aalen. 1960.

Reinhold Ebertin, Kombination der Gestirneinflusse (KdG), Erfurt, 1935, Aalen, 1945, 1950, 1961; English: *The Combination of Stellar Influences* (CSI), revised and enlarged, Aalen,

1972; also English supplement to CSI, Aalen, 1970. Reinhold Ebertin, editor of the journal, *Kosmobiologie*, started

1928.
Alfred Witte, Regelwerk der Planetenbilder, Hamburg, 1928/1935.
The Graphic 45°-Ephemerides, published by the Ebertin-Verlag, Aalen, since 1948. For explanations see Sternenbahnen.
Theodor Landscheidt, Fixstern-Ephemeride, Aalen, 1963; also a new textbook, *Fixed Stars*, by Ebertin-Hoffmann, Aalen, 1971.
Reinhold Ebertin, *Kosmopsychologie*, Aalen, 1950.
Jean Gebser, Ursprung und Gegenwart, Bd. 1, *Das Fundament der aperspektiven Welt*, Stuttgart, 1949.
IKN-International Nomenclature: see CSI, p. 28, presenting a listing of internationally agreed abbreviations for planets, signs, etc,
Prof. R. Tomaschek, Kosmische Kraftfelder und astrale Einflusse, Aalen, 1959; see also *In Search*, Winter 1959/60, pp. 84-91 (New York) for English summary of this work.
Astro-Addiator, DM 35.
In order to be better able to judge the nature of the heavenly bodies, a table has been published in the book *Transits*, p. 36 of the English edition. The author has stressed since the 1952 edition that there is no reason why squares and oppositions should not be favourable; it is the "nature" of the heavenly bodies and not the type of angle formed that is of significance.
Hermann Grimm, Goethe, Detmod, 1948.
Wolfgang Gotz, Goethe, sein Leben in Selbstzeugnissen, Berlin, 1947.
Ref. 44 see Ref. 17
Reinhold Ebertin, *Vorschau durch Direktionen*, 1st edition, Erfurt, 1930. latest edition, Aalen, 1953.
Reinhold Ebertin, *Table of Events*, Aalen, 1971: tables for correction of birth-time and for prognostication.
Theodor Landscheidt, *Hinweise auf die Gultigkeit der 45°-+135°-Aspekte.*
Reinhold Ebertin, *Die kosmische Ehe*, 1933/1950.

Reinhold Ebertin, *Die anatomischen Entsprechungen der Tier-kreisgrade*, Aalen, 1959, revised and enlarged 1971.
Frhr. v. Klockler, *Astrologie als Erfahrungswissenschaft*, Leipzig, 1926.
Frhr. v. Klockler, *Berufsbegabung und Berufschicksal*, Leipzig, 1928.
Michel Gauquelin, *L'influence des astres*, Paris, 1955; see also "The Cosmic Clocks", Regency, Chicago, 1967.
Arthur Hubscher, *Philosophen der Gegenwart*, Munich, 1949.
Reinhold Ebertin, *Gesicherte Schnelldiagnose*, Aalen, 1959/1972, English edition, *Rapid and Reliable Analysis*, Aalen, 1970.

TABLE OF EQUIVALENTS

Sign	360°	90°	45°	Sign	360°	90°	45°	Sign	360°	90°	45°
01° ♈ =	001 =	01 =	01	01° ♊ =	061 =	61 =	16	01° ♌ =	121 =	31 =	31
02	002	02	02	02	062	62	17	02	122	32	32
03	003	03	03	03	063	63	18	03	123	33	33
04	004	04	04	04	064	64	19	04	124	34	34
05	005	05	05	05	065	65	20	05	125	35	35
06	006	06	06	06	066	66	21	06	126	36	36
07	007	07	07	07	067	67	22	07	127	37	37
08	008	08	08	08	068	68	23	08	128	38	38
09	009	09	09	09	069	69	24	09	129	39	39
10	010	10	10	10	070	70	25	10	130	40	40
11	011	11	11	11	071	71	26	11	131	41	41
12	012	12	12	12	072	72	27	12	132	42	42
13	013	13	13	13	073	73	28	13	133	43	43
14	014	14	14	14	074	74	29	14	134	44	44
15	015	15	15	15	075	75	30	15	135	45	45
16	016	16	16	16	076	76	31	16	136	46	1
17	017	17	17	17	077	77	32	17	137	47	2
18	018	18	18	18	078	78	33	18	138	48	3
19	019	19	19	19	079	79	34	19	139	49	4
20	020	20	20	20	080	80	35	20	140	50	5
21	021	21	21	21	081	81	36	21	141	51	6
22	022	22	22	22	082	82	37	22	142	52	7
23	023	23	23	23	083	83	38	23	143	53	8
24	024	24	24	24	084	84	39	24	144	54	9
25	025	25	25	25	085	85	40	25	145	55	10
26	026	26	26	26	086	86	41	26	146	56	11
27	027	27	27	27	087	87	42	27	147	57	12
28	028	28	28	28	088	88	43	28	148	58	13
29	029	29	29	29	089	89	44	29	149	59	14
00 ♉	030	30	30	00 ♋	090	00	00	00 ♍	150	60	15
01	031	31	31	01	091	01	01	01	151	61	16
02	032	32	32	02	092	02	02	02	152	62	17
03	033	33	33	03	093	03	03	03	153	63	18
04	034	34	34	04	094	04	04	04	154	64	19
05	035	35	35	05	095	05	05	05	155	65	20
06	036	36	36	06	096	06	06	06	156	66	21
07	037	37	37	07	097	07	07	07	157	67	22
08	038	38	38	08	098	08	08	08	158	68	23
09	039	39	39	09	099	09	09	09	159	69	24
10	040	40	40	10	100	10	10	10	160	70	25
11	041	41	41	11	101	11	11	11	161	71	26
12	042	42	42	12	102	12	12	12	162	72	27
13	043	43	43	13	103	13	13	13	163	73	28
14	044	44	44	14	104	14	14	14	164	74	29
15	045	45	00	15	105	15	15	15	165	75	30
16	046	46	01	16	106	16	16	16	166	76	31
17	047	47	02	17	107	17	17	17	167	77	32
18	048	48	03	18	108	18	18	18	168	78	33
19	049	49	04	19	109	19	19	19	169	79	34
20	050	50	05	20	110	20	20	20	170	80	35
21	051	51	06	21	111	21	21	21	171	81	36
22	052	52	07	22	112	22	22	22	172	82	37
23	053	53	08	23	113	23	23	23	173	83	38
24	054	54	09	24	114	24	24	24	174	84	39
25	055	55	10	25	115	25	25	25	175	85	40
26	056	56	11	26	116	26	26	26	176	86	41
27	057	57	12	27	117	27	27	27	177	87	42
28	058	58	13	28	118	28	28	28	178	88	43
29	059	59	14	29	119	29	29	29	179	89	44
00 ♊	060	60	15	00 ♌	120	30	30	00 ♎	180	00	00

TABLE OF EQUIVALENTS

Sign	360°	90°	45°	Sign	360°	90°	45°	Sign	360°	90°	45°
01° ♎ =	181 =	01 =	01	01° ♐ =	241 =	61 =	16	01° ♒ =	301 =	31 =	31
02	182	02	02	02	242	62	17	02	302	32	32
03	183	03	03	03	243	63	18	03	303	33	33
04	184	04	04	04	244	64	19	04	304	34	34
05	185	05	05	05	245	65	20	05	305	35	35
06	186	06	06	06	246	66	21	06	306	36	36
07	187	07	07	07	247	67	22	07	307	37	37
08	188	08	08	08	248	68	23	08	308	38	38
09	189	09	09	09	249	69	24	09	309	39	39
10	190	10	10	10	250	70	25	10	310	40	40
11	191	11	11	11	251	71	26	11	311	41	41
12	192	12	12	12	252	72	27	12	312	42	42
13	193	13	13	13	253	73	28	13	313	43	43
14	194	14	14	14	254	74	29	14	314	44	44
15	195	15	15	15	255	75	30	15	315	45	00
16	196	16	16	16	256	76	31	16	316	46	01
17	197	17	17	17	257	77	32	17	317	47	02
18	198	18	18	18	258	78	33	18	318	48	03
19	199	19	19	19	259	79	34	19	319	49	04
20	200	20	20	20	260	80	35	20	320	50	05
21	201	21	21	21	261	81	36	21	321	51	06
22	202	22	22	22	262	82	37	22	322	52	07
23	203	23	23	23	263	83	38	23	323	53	08
24	204	24	24	24	264	84	39	24	324	54	09
25	205	25	25	25	265	85	40	25	325	55	10
26	206	26	26	26	266	86	41	26	326	56	11
27	207	27	27	27	267	87	42	27	327	57	12
28	208	28	28	28	268	88	43	28	328	58	13
29	209	29	29	29	269	89	44	29	329	59	14
00 ♏	210	30	30	00 ♑	270	00	00	00 ♓	330	60	15
01	211	31	31	01	271	01	01	01	331	61	16
02	212	32	32	02	272	02	02	02	332	62	17
03	213	33	33	03	273	03	03	03	333	63	18
04	214	34	34	04	274	04	04	04	334	64	19
05	215	35	35	05	275	05	05	05	335	65	20
06	216	36	36	06	276	06	06	06	336	66	21
07	217	37	37	07	277	07	07	07	337	67	22
08	218	38	38	08	278	08	08	08	338	68	23
09	219	39	39	09	279	09	09	09	339	69	24
10	220	40	40	10	280	10	10	10	340	70	25
11	221	41	41	11	281	11	11	11	341	71	26
12	222	42	42	12	282	12	12	12	342	72	27
13	223	43	43	13	283	13	13	13	343	73	28
14	224	44	44	14	284	14	14	14	344	74	29
15	225	45	00	15	285	15	15	15	345	75	30
16	226	46	01	16	286	16	16	16	346	76	31
17	227	47	02	17	287	17	17	17	347	77	32
18	228	48	03	18	288	18	18	18	348	78	33
19	229	49	04	19	289	19	19	19	349	79	34
20	230	50	05	20	290	20	20	20	350	80	35
21	231	51	06	21	291	21	21	21	351	81	36
22	232	52	07	22	292	22	22	22	352	82	37
23	233	53	08	23	293	23	23	23	353	83	38
24	234	54	09	24	294	24	24	24	354	84	39
25	235	55	10	25	295	25	25	25	355	85	40
26	236	56	11	26	296	26	26	26	356	86	41
27	237	57	12	27	297	27	27	27	357	87	42
28	238	58	13	28	298	28	28	28	258	88	43
29	239	59	14	29	299	29	29	29	259	89	44
00 ♐	240	60	15	00 ♒	300	30	30	00 ♈	000	00	00

Lightning Source UK Ltd.
Milton Keynes UK
UKHW011244310120
357954UK00001B/125